FOLLOWING GOD
DISCIPLESHIP SERIES
BIBLE STUDY

An informative **12 WEEK BIBLE STUDY** of life principles for today, and the Christian's walk.

Transforming the Heart

A BIBLICAL FRAMEWORK FOR DISCIPLESHIP AND COUNSELING

MENDY CLARK DEd. Min.

AMG
PUBLISHERS

Transforming the Heart

A BIBLICAL FRAMEWORK
FOR DISCIPLESHIP
AND COUNSELING

AMG
PUBLISHERS

MENDY CLARK DEd. Min.

May this workbook be a footstool at His feet!

He chose. He prepared.
He gave the ministry.
He empowers the ministry.

This is the Lord's doing, and it is marvelous in our eyes!

Glory to God!

CONTENTS

PREFACE

> "I will *instruct* you and *teach* you in the way you should
> go; I will *counsel* you with My eye upon you."
>
> (Ps. 32:8, emphasis added)

I distinctly remember the day that the Lord illuminated this verse. Initially, the Lord spoke these words to David, in regard to sin. However, the underlying principle that God is a God who instructs, teaches, and counsels His children particularly captured my attention. This occurred while I was praying about whether the Lord wanted me to take the position I had been offered as the dean of women at the Christian school where I was already teaching Bible. As I read the verse, I sensed the Holy Spirit calling my attention to the verbs and their order. I began to realize the Lord was giving me His answer to the question I had been asking in reference to His will for my life. I had been instructing and teaching His Word. Now, He would add the counseling aspect to the ministry He was entrusting to me.

Years later, He would illuminate that same verse as I began to seek His will in regard to furthering my education. I was at the crossroads concerning the decision whether to pursue a master's degree in biblical counseling or to continue with emphasis on the Word in religious education. I had never wanted to be a counselor; however, the Lord kept sending women of all ages for counsel. I noticed this occurred after I taught the Word. As the years have passed, the Lord has shown me that counseling is a natural by-product of teaching His Word. I will never forget when He impressed on my heart that I would counsel by using the Word of God. Therefore, I realized that I would need to know His Word, and so I focused the rest of my biblical education on the Word.

As I was finishing my doctoral dissertation, the professor who served as my chair, Dr. Patricia Nason, said, "Mendy, I think this information needs to be written in a book and published for discipleship in the church." My first thought was *You have got to be kidding me! I have no desire to be an author, not to mention the fact that I never want to write another word again after doing this dissertation!* But after only a few months, spurred on by the insistence of my daughters and some of the women I disciple, I sensed again the leading of the Lord to put my dissertation into a workbook for laymen in the church who have a heart to disciple others. As I prayerfully asked the Lord for guidance, once again the Holy

Spirit illuminated Psalm 32:8. He used this verse to serve as the catalyst for this workbook, emphasizing again the verbs and their order—*instruct*, *teach*, and *counsel*—along with His ever-faithful promise that His eye would be on me as I surrendered my will and obeyed His leading. And so here is the fruit of the past thirty-plus years of personal study, struggle, and growth as His disciple. My prayer is that everyone who picks up this book will see *Him*, for there is no one sweeter to behold!

CHAPTER 1

THE INTRODUCTION

"Like newborn babes, long for the *pure* milk of the word, that by
it [the Word] you may *grow* in respect to salvation."
(1 Pet. 2:2, emphasis added)

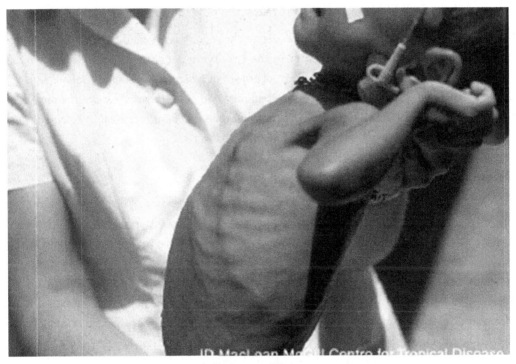

Failure to Thrive

THE NECESSITY OF DISCIPLESHIP: THE PROBLEM

In the early 1900s, the term *failure to thrive* became a medical diagnosis. Failure to thrive is a medical condition first observed and diagnosed in institutionalized infants. Symptoms include rapid weight loss, listlessness, and depression, resulting in subsequent death. Studies were conducted to answer why nearly 100 percent of institutionalized infants were either sick or dying. In 1945 Hungarian psychiatrist René Spitz led the research. According to *The Encyclopedia of Nursing Research*, "Dr. Spitz described depression, growth failure, and malnutrition in sixty-one foundling home infants. He proposed a lack of emotional stimulation and the absence of a mother figure as the main contributors to infant growth failure."[1] Spitz concluded his research by saying that with adequate attention, love, and stimulation, the infants would not only survive but thrive.

Since Spitz's research, many advances have occurred with regard to this medical syndrome. According to *The Gale Encyclopedia of Children's Health*, "failure to thrive can be divided into two main categories: Organic, which includes physical abnormalities, and Inorganic, caused by a caregiver's neglect."[2] Children in abusive or neglectful families are at a higher risk for failure to thrive. Understanding this concept to be true, that malnutrition is the most common cause should come as no surprise.[3] The analogy of the physical malady of failure to thrive can also be true in the spiritual realm as it relates to the Inorganic category, which involves the caregiver's negligence. Just as the institutionalized infants were lacking proper nourishment and nurturing, people within the church are experiencing a deficit in the proper nourishment from the Word and nurturing from others in discipleship. However, the Organic category, which includes physical anomalies, can be eliminated because of the biblical fact that those who are born spiritually are given all that is necessary for life and godliness at the time of salvation (2 Pet. 1:3).

Looking at the signs and symptoms of failure to thrive, one is inclined to ask the following questions in relation to men and women in the twenty-first-century church: *Are the men and women in the church experiencing spiritual growth as biblically outlined in 1 John 2:12-14? If so, is this discipleship ministry interconnected, nurtured, and thriving? Or are the men and women who attend like the orphans in the institution—malnourished, weak, neglected, not growing, and unable to thrive?*

Discipleship Defined

In light of this information, the purpose of this workbook is to assess, diagnose, and offer a treatment through biblical principles to the affected ministry within the church—namely, the discipleship of men and women. If the Great Physician were to give the body of Christ a spiritual examination with regard to discipleship, would the diagnosis read, "Nurtured or Neglected: Thriving or Failing to Thrive?" Sadly, many in the church believe that discipleship is a program. Bible professor and author Jim Berg states, "Biblical discipleship is not primarily a program. It is a certain kind of relationship between two believers with a very specific spiritual goal in mind. Discipleship is helping another believer make biblical change toward Christlikeness—helping others in the sanctification process."[4] Likewise, Bible professor Max Barnett agrees, stating, "The focus on knowing Christ in a progressive way and then making Him known to others isn't a program to go through, but a lifestyle to develop."[5] In other words, discipleship is the process of allowing the Lord to apply His words to the heart (mind, will, and emotion) with the same results—if only we will allow Him.

I am writing this workbook because for me, discipleship is personal. Despite having been a Christian for twenty-five years, I was woefully lacking in training regarding discipleship in God's Word. Basically, I spent twenty-five years as a spiritual baby because I was not nourished with the Word of God.

As a former registered coronary intensive care nurse, I understand the importance of knowing how to make an accurate assessment and diagnosis and to treat physical abnormalities of the heart. This training has been invaluable in preserving lives. Similarly, when the Lord called me at the age of thirty-one to exchange "physical hearts" for "spiritual hearts," the necessity to train became imperative. Learning to make an accurate assessment and diagnosis and to treat spiritual issues of the heart requires supernatural help from the only One who really knows the heart (Jer. 17:9–10). Unlike the physical heart, which has many avenues of cardiac drugs and treatments available in a health crisis, the spiritual heart has only one physician and one treatment—the Word of God.

This workbook is the culmination of many years of training to be able to make biblical assessments and diagnoses, and to treat the spiritual immaturity of many of the men and women in the local church. Despite spending many years in the church, men and women are voicing their concerns about spiritual immaturity. The problem lies not only in a lack of spiritual maturity but also in a deficit in the training for those who are trained and equipped to point others toward spiritual maturity. In essence, the men and women in the church are being neglected rather than nurtured in the Word of God.

One of my personal goals is to equip women's ministries throughout local churches and seminaries to become Word-driven and not event-oriented. My prayer is that women, in particular, would become an entity functioning under biblical authority that is respected because of its theological grounding, rather than being driven by emotion. My desire is to see the women of the church provide an effective ministry in which the goal of Bible study is transformation rather than mere information.

So where do we start in this process of discipleship? I was asked this question by a precious friend, whom I had the privilege of discipling. She had been asked by another woman in the church to disciple her because the woman had witnessed such an evident transformation in my friend. As I explained the process to my friend, and remembered the counsel of my professor, the Lord impressed upon my mind that this would be the flow of the workbook.

The first topic to address must be salvation, for no one can disciple someone who is lost. Second, once salvation is a settled issue, a biblical model is needed to help "diagnose" or determine where the individual is in his or her walk. The diagnostic tool presented in this workbook is based on the spiritual levels of maturity seen in 1 John 2:12–14. Based on the biblical "diagnosis," God's Spirit will use God's Word to determine the treatment. For example, if the Spirit of truth reveals through the Word of God that an individual is a spiritual baby, the individual will need help in learning how to overcome the enemy as well as what it means to have the Word of God abide within them on a consistent basis. This will provide the basis for the flow of the workbook.

Interwoven throughout this workbook are messages addressed to both counselor and counselee. This workbook was not designed to do alone. It has been created to aid in the process of one-on-one discipleship. If you are wondering if this workbook is for you, consider the following questions:

Would you like to be personally discipled by using just the Word of God?
Would you like to know how to use God's Word to disciple someone else?

Would you know where to begin or how to proceed if asked to disciple another person?

Would you like to know how to counsel someone who is struggling or stagnant in his or her spiritual walk, just using the Word of God?

Would you like to know how to help someone learn how to study the Word on his or her own?

If you answered yes to any of these questions, this workbook was designed for you![*]

THE NECESSITY OF DISCIPLESHIP: THE SOLUTION

> His divine power has *granted to us everything pertaining to life and godliness*, through the true knowledge of Him who called us by His own glory and excellence." (2 Pet. 1:3, emphasis added)

Clearly from Scripture we see that because of Christ Jesus and His divine power, we have been given everything we need "pertaining to life and godliness." Why then do we constantly look elsewhere? What are we building on the foundation of Christ, and is this important in the process of sanctification? Have we been deceived? The apostle Paul warns the believer, "According to the grace of God which was given to me, as a wise master builder I laid a foundation, and another is building upon it. But let each man be careful how he builds upon it. For no man can lay a foundation other than the one which is laid, which is Jesus Christ" (1 Cor. 3:10–11).

Do you see the warning? "Let each man be careful how he builds" on the foundation of Christ Jesus. In other words, be careful not only that you are being discipled but also *how* you are being discipled. If you are spiritually weak and being overcome by the enemy, biblical counseling becomes a necessary part of the process. More than likely, you are spiritually weak and being overcome because you are deceived. The most troubling fact about deception is that you can be walking in deception without knowing it. Only the Spirit of God using the Word can expose the lies of deception. We know that truth is the opposite of deception. Therefore, we must begin with a biblical definition of the word *truth*.

1. Look at the following verses of Scripture to biblically define *truth*. Who/what is truth in the following passages of Scripture?

    a. Isaiah 65:16– _____

    b. John 14:6– _____

    c. John 16:13– _____

---

[*] As you proceed, please be advised that this workbook has been designed using the New American Standard Bible (1977 edition). This information will prove helpful in order for your answers to align with the blanks provided.

1 John 5:6–7 – _____

d. John 17:17 – _____

Psalm 119:151 – _____

Ephesians 1:13 – _____

2 Timothy 2:15 – _____

2. Now, define the *truth* using Scripture. _____

3. Look at 1 Timothy 3:15 and record the church's relation to the truth.

a. The church is called the _____ and the _____ of the truth.

b. What does a pillar do? _____

c. What are we, the church, called to do with the truth? _____

Definition of Deception

Discipleship and biblical counseling cannot occur without the Father, the Lord Jesus, His Spirit, and the Word of God. These are the necessary elements that make up the truth. To identify areas of deception, we must personally and experientially know the truth. But what exactly is deception? First and foremost, it is the exact opposite of truth! The serpent was able to deceive Eve. Likewise, he is still in the business of deception. Deception is when we say one thing but do something different.

Because I am a visual learner I like to define it this way:

The Picture of Deception

This is what I *say* I believe, BUT this is what I *do*! If the two do not match, a person is living/walking in deception. The **truth** about what you believe is **what you do!**

Therefore, the role of the human counselor/discipler is to point others to the truth. The biblical counselor's job is to listen for things that do not align with the truth of God and His Word and point out any inconsistencies between what they say and what they do. And then point them to the truth in God's Word! **If Scripture is true—and it is—then what exactly have we been given for life and godliness?**

Let's spend some time looking at what the Scriptures say we have been given in regard to the truth and our souls/hearts.

The Lord Jesus Christ

1. Look at 1 Peter 2:25 and record what Jesus is called in this verse.

   _____ and _____ of our **souls** (hearts).

   Why do you think Jesus is called the Shepherd and Guardian of our souls?

   a. What does our Shepherd do for His sheep? _____

   _____

   b. Now look at John 10:4, 10. What do you learn about the sheep in regard to their Shepherd?

   _____

   c. Why do you think the Lord Jesus is called the "Guardian" of our souls (hearts)?

   _____

No one knew the reality of this truth more than Peter. Let's explore why. A study on the apostle Peter in the Gospels looks very different from the Peter we see in his first epistle. Let's look at a passage from the Gospels and discover why Peter was uniquely qualified to call Jesus "the Shepherd and Guardian of your souls."

2. Look at Luke 22:31–34 and answer the following questions.

   a. What do we learn from Jesus in regard to Peter from verse 31? _____

   _____

   b. What did Jesus do for Peter in verse 32? _____

   c. What specifically did Jesus pray for in verse 32? _____

   This is interesting, isn't it? Jesus prayed specifically for Peter's faith! I wonder if that is a prayer we should be praying for those we love as well as ourselves.

   d. What did Jesus know about Peter in verse 32? _____

e. What did Jesus encourage Peter to do once he "turned again"?

_____

f. What was Peter's reply to Jesus in verse 33?

_____

_____

g. What did the Lord tell Peter he would do in verse 34?

_____

The message delivered was, in essence, "You will fail." But Peter, instead of crying out for help, chose not to believe that this was the truth.

3. Now, let's look at Luke 22:54–62 and answer the following questions.

  a. Where is Peter in regard to Jesus according to verse 54?

  b. Where is Peter sitting in verse 55?

  c. When questioned by the servant girl, what did Peter do in verse 57?

  d. Questioned again by another who saw Peter, what was Peter's reply?

_____

Scripture states, "After about an hour had passed, another man began to insist, saying, 'Certainly this man also was with Him, for he is a Galilean too'" (verse 59).

  e. How did Peter respond to this man according to verse 60?

_____

  f. What happened immediately after Peter's third denial according to verse 60?

_____

  g. Now, carefully record the sequence of events in verses 61–62. Note the order!

    1) The Lord _____ and _____ at Peter.

    2) Peter remembered the _____ of the _____, how He had told him, "Before a cock crows today, you will _____ Me three times."

    3) And he [Peter] went out and _____.

  h. Now, let's revisit 1 Peter 2:25. Why would Peter be uniquely qualified to call Jesus the "Shepherd and Guardian" of our souls? Any thoughts?

_____

_____

Peter learned in a very real and personal way that Jesus truly was the "Shepherd and Guardian" of his soul. We, like Peter, need to understand that the enemy places a target on our souls (minds, wills, and emotions). Only Jesus, the Good Shepherd, can guide, guard, and graze our souls. We, like Peter, need to learn to recognize His voice as He speaks through His Word and obey His voice. Peter's epistles prove that he learned this lesson well. Have you?

The Holy Spirit

Now we want to examine the role of the Holy Spirit in regard to our hearts/souls.

1. Look at Isaiah 11:2 and list the characteristics of the Holy Spirit. He is called the following:

   a. **The Spirit of the LORD**

   b. The spirit of _____

   c. The spirit of _____

   d. The spirit of _____

   e. The spirit of _____

   f. The spirit of _____

   g. The spirit of _____

Note: Look at the characteristics that directly affect the heart. What do these characteristics have to do with the heart of mankind?

_____

_____

The heart is the mind, will, and emotions. The mind controls what we think, which will in turn affect what we do and how we feel. As we think about the characteristics of the Holy Spirit and man's heart, consider the words of 1 Corinthians 2:14: "But a natural man does not accept the things of the Spirit of God; for they are foolishness to him, and he cannot understand them, because they are spiritually appraised." The natural man is a reference to the man without the Spirit of God.

2. What role, then, does the Holy Spirit play in regard to our hearts?

_____

   a. Now look at Ezekiel 36:26–27. What is the role of the Holy Spirit in these passages of Scripture as it relates to the heart of man? _____

_____

   b. Likewise, Jesus, speaking to His disciples about the Holy Spirit, whom He would send, said, "But when He, the Spirit of truth, comes, He will guide you into all the truth; for He will not speak on His own initiative, but whatever He hears, He will speak" (John 16:13).

3. Look at John 16:13 above and answer the following questions.

   a. What does the Lord Jesus specifically call the Holy Spirit? _____

   b. What will God's Spirit do when He comes?

   _____   _____   _____

Do you see that when the Holy Spirit comes, He guides, hears, and speaks? Thankfully, the Spirit of truth is still guiding us to all the truth and speaking today! If you will allow Him, He will guide you to all the truth and speak to you today as well. But what will He use?

The Word of God

Jesus, when praying for His disciples in His High Priestly Prayer, asked the Father, "Sanctify them in the truth; Thy word is truth" (John 17:17). The Spirit of God is obligated only to the Word of God. Men and women alike are being overcome by the evil one because they are deceived and do not know the Word of God. Think back to the garden. When Eve told the serpent what God said, did she get it right? Look at the following passages that record the specific facts regarding the Word of God.

1. James 1:21b– _____

_____

2. 1 Peter 2:2– _____

_____

_____

Oftentimes, when I am studying the Word of God, I like to divide the text into two parts: God's part and my part. Clearly, God's part in the revelation of truth is in His person. He ALWAYS does His part. My part, on the other hand, is to respond to the truth of His Word by the power of His Spirit within me. Therefore, my part requires faith. Remember, faith is a gift from God (Eph. 2:8), from the Author (Source) and Perfecter of faith (Heb. 12:2). Therefore, God is not requiring anything from us that He has not first given.

The Counselee's Faith

Over the last thirty-plus years of studying the Word, one thing is abundantly clear. From Genesis to Revelation, the only correct response to God's Word is faith. No matter where I go in Scripture, the message is the same—the disciple of Jesus Christ is to exercise faith/belief in God's Word.

1. Let's look at Hebrews 11:6 and record the verse. Note the importance of faith.

_____

_____

Did you see the importance placed on faith? Hebrews 11:6a states, "Without faith it is **impossible** to please [God]" (emphasis added). But what about the verb *believe*? Didn't Jesus say, "Truly, truly, I say to you, he who believes has eternal life" (John 6:47)? It might interest you to know that the words *faith* and *believe* come from the same Greek root word. Although they look nothing alike in the English language, in the Greek they have the same meaning but are different parts of speech. *Faith* is a noun and *believe* is a verb. The definition for both is threefold:

1. Firm conviction of God's Word—God's Spirit uses God's Word to convict our hearts

2. Personal surrender of my will to God's Word

3. Obedience to God's Word[6]

Today, many "profess" faith but do not "possess" it. Faith is more than just a firm conviction for God's Word, which, by itself, amounts to head knowledge. Although necessary, and the order matters, God's Spirit uses the Word to convict. However, there must also be a personal surrender of our wills to God's will (Word). This is where the internal struggle is fought and won. The external evidence will be in the outward obedience to His Word. All three components are necessary for saving faith.

Now I know what some of you might be thinking: the Pharisees had memorized God's Word, and they were outwardly obedient. BUT the missing factor involved the surrender of the will. Jesus, quoting Isaiah, described the Pharisees this way: "This people honor Me with their lips, but their heart is far away from Me" (Matt. 15:8). The Pharisees prided themselves on knowing and obeying God's Word. But if Jesus said, "Their heart is far away from Me," the surrender of their wills is the missing factor.

In a counseling situation, if the Spirit of truth reveals an area in counselees' lives where they are covering, hiding, or blaming, they must be willing to surrender their wills to God's will (Word) and walk in obedience to His Word. If counselees are not willing to do so, there will be no freedom gained from the enemy and their hearts will not be completely healed.

4. We know that Jesus is the Author or Source of faith, and the believer is given this gift at salvation (Eph. 2:8), but where else do we get the faith of Hebrews 11:6?

   Look at Romans 10:17 and record the verse. _____

The Human Counselor/Discipler

I learned a long time ago that I am not the Counselor and this is not a program! Each person is different, and the Holy Spirit is the one leading. I usually have no clue where He will lead, and more than likely, you will not know either. And that's a great place to be—totally dependent on His leading, always pointing to the Lord of the Word and the Word of the Lord.

One of the first things I tell women who come for spiritual counsel is that I cannot even set myself free—much less them. After I finish teaching the Scriptures, a woman will inevitably come for more counseling after class. Years ago, unfortunately, I thought I had to help the women I counseled come up with the correct answer or figure out what they needed. This led to a heaviness within my spirit and a load that I could not bear. I would find myself actually dreading the counseling appointment. Thankfully, this was never the Lord's intention, and in His kindness, He revealed that to me. I learned to trust the illuminating power of the Holy Spirit, who uses the Word of God to lead to truth and shine light in areas of the heart that need healing, areas that only He can see. Therefore, I have learned that the most important instruction throughout the entire counseling session is "Ask the Lord Jesus to lead you by the power of the Holy Spirit, who is the Spirit of truth." After a time of listening and waiting on Him to lead, we can proceed to what He deems necessary. Without His guidance, there is no need to meet. The human counselor is merely the one pointing to the Lord of the Word and the Word of the Lord through the power of the Holy Spirit. In essence, we are to be the pillar and support of the truth!

In conclusion, consider the following quotation from pastor and author John MacArthur, as he succinctly defines true biblical counseling. He states:

> The truly Christian counselor must be doing soul work in the realm of the deep things of the Word and the Spirit, not fooling around in the shallows of behavior modification. Why should believers choose to do behavior modification when we have the tools for spiritual transformation (like a surgeon wreaking havoc with a butter knife instead of using a scalpel)? The most skilled counselor is the one who most carefully, prayerfully, and faithfully applies the divine spiritual resources to the process of sanctification, shaping another into the image of Jesus Christ.[7]

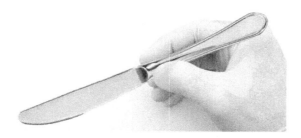

Now that we understand that we have been given everything we need for life and godliness, let's look specifically at how to overcome the enemy using the biblical foundation and framework found in the Word. You may be asking, "So where do we begin?" We will begin at the beginning, where sin entered and man fell. Where the enemy was speaking and man chose to listen to his voice rather than the voice of the Lord God. This is still the most important truth to learn in overcoming the enemy today! Overcoming the enemy begins with learning to identify the voices/thoughts within your head!

NOTES

CHAPTER 2

KEY DISCIPLESHIP DOCTRINAL TRUTHS AND TERMS

"Sanctify them in truth; Thy word is truth."

(John 17:17)

To have a full understanding of this workbook, you will need to have working definitions of some key words used throughout. The following list of terms must be identified and understood as you proceed: the Holy Spirit and His sanctifying work, Illumination, the Heart/Soul, Faith/Believe, and Repentance.

THE LORD'S PRAYER AND INSTRUCTIONS FOR SANCTIFICATION

In His High Priestly Prayer just hours before His crucifixion, Jesus prayed to the Father not only for His disciples but also for every disciple who would follow Him (John 17:17). This prayer was prayed for you, if you are a disciple of Christ. If you look closely, you will discover that it is more than a request. The Master Teacher is giving us instructions for discipleship. In His prayer, Jesus is addressing *how* one is to be sanctified. Sanctification is a process of being discipled by the Spirit of truth, using the Word of truth.

But what does this look like in the life of a disciple? There is much being said about the person and work of the Holy Spirit today. Some of the things out there today are heretical. In his book titled *Strange Fire*, pastor and author John MacArthur candidly addresses the situation:

> On the one hand, some mainstream evangelicals are guilty of neglecting the Holy Spirit altogether. For them, He has become the forgotten member of the Trinity—as they attempt to grow through their own cleverness rather than His power. . . . On the other hand, the modern Pentecostal and Charismatic Movements have pushed the pendulum to the opposite extreme. They have fostered an unhealthy preoccupation with supposed manifestations of the Holy Spirit's power.[8]

With this in mind, a biblical view of the Holy Spirit and His work is necessary to understand this workbook and process of discipleship.

THE HOLY SPIRIT AND HIS SANCTIFYING WORK

First and foremost, the Holy Spirit is the third person of the Trinity. He is first mentioned in Genesis 1:2 and is involved in the creation of the universe along with the Father, who spoke things into existence (Gen. 1:3; Heb. 11:3), and the Son (Col. 1:15–17).

According to Scripture, He has various names that distinguish His work and His character. In Isaiah 11:2, He is called the "Spirit of the LORD" who rested upon the Lord Jesus during His earthly ministry. He is also called the Spirit of wisdom, the Spirit of understanding, the Spirit of counsel, the Spirit of strength, the Spirit of knowledge, and the Spirit of "the fear of the LORD."

He is called the Spirit of God (1 Cor. 3:16), the Spirit of Christ (Rom. 8:9), the Spirit of truth (John 16:13), the Spirit of grace (Heb. 10:29), the Spirit of glory (1 Pet. 4:14), the Spirit of life (Rom. 8:2), the Spirit of wisdom and revelation (Eph. 1:17), the Helper (John 14:26), the Spirit of promise (Acts 1:4–5), the Spirit of adoption (Rom. 8:15), the Spirit of holiness (Rom. 1:4), and the Spirit of faith (2 Cor. 4:13).

His sanctifying work is evident in the Word. In his book *Wilmington's Guide to the Bible*, author and Bible teacher Harold Wilmington identifies five distinct ministries of the Holy Spirit in the life of a believer, specifically:

1. The Holy Spirit regenerates the believing sinner (John 3:3–7; Titus 3:5; James 1:18; 1 Pet. 1:23).

2. The Holy Spirit baptizes the believing sinner (Rom. 6:3–4; 1 Cor. 12:13; Gal. 3:27; Eph. 4:4–5; Col. 2:12).

3. The Holy Spirit indwells the believing sinner (John 7:37–39; 14:16, 20; Rom. 8:9; 1 Cor. 2:12; 3:16; 2 Cor. 5:17; Gal. 5:16–18; Eph. 3:16; 1 John 3:24).

4. The Holy Spirit seals the believing sinner (2 Cor. 1:22; 5:5; Eph. 1:13–14; 4:30).

5. The Holy Spirit leads and fills the believing sinner (Gal. 5:16–18; Eph. 5:18).[9]

According to Wilmington, the first four ministries cannot be lost or altered because they are completely a work of God for salvation. However, the fifth ministry, the filling of the Spirit, can vary in the life of a believer and is dependent on one's obedience to the Word of God.

As we progress through this workbook, you will see the emphasis on the Spirit of God and the Word of God, for the two are inseparable! But because of the mounting heresy today, I feel as if I must give you a couple of words of caution before you proceed:

1. The author of the Word will not speak contrary to the Word (2 Pet. 1:20–21).

   Therefore, *the Spirit of God will not say anything contrary to the Word of God!*

2. There is no new revelation. The canon of Scripture is closed! We are not to add to or subtract from the Word of God (Deut. 4:2; Rev. 22:18).

For example, because the Holy Spirit is the Spirit of truth and He leads us to truth (John 16:13), He will not say anything to us that is contrary to the Word He inspired (2 Pet. 1:20–21). He is the One who illumines the Word, but there will not be any new revelation or prophecy. Therefore, when the workbook suggests praying and asking the Holy Spirit to guide you to truth, you must understand that He will counsel through the written Word of God.

THE DOCTRINE OF ILLUMINATION

Throughout the workbook, you will see the terms *illuminate*, *illuminating*, and *illumines*. These terms must be understood in light of the Word and the power and work of the Holy Spirit. Paul explains this doctrine biblically:

> But a natural man does not accept the things of the Spirit of God; for they are foolishness to him, and he cannot understand them, because they are spiritually appraised. But he who is spiritual appraises all things, yet he himself is appraised by no man. For who has known the mind of the Lord, that he should instruct Him? But we have the mind of Christ. (1 Cor. 2:14–16)

The natural man is the man without the Spirit of God. The man without the Spirit of God will never understand the meaning of God's Word. In fact, it will appear as foolishness to him. Therefore, the Spirit is necessary to understand the meaning of the Word. In essence, it takes God to understand God.

It is important to understand the meaning of illumination because of the ongoing abuse of the Spirit's work and the Word. There are many today professing or "prophesying" to have a "word from the Lord" that looks nothing like His Word or is the Word of God taken out of context. We must be careful not to mishandle the Word of God by making it say something God did not say. Helping us understand the meaning of the term *illumination*, the late apologist Carl Henry stated, "By the illumination of the Spirit, believers are aided in their understanding of particular passages of Scripture, **but it is Scripture that the Spirit illumines, and not simply the believer**" (emphasis added).[10]

Further expounding, Henry explained, "God intends that Scripture should function in our lives as His Spirit-illumined Word. It is the Spirit who opens man's being to a keen personal awareness of God's revelation. The Spirit empowers us to receive and appropriate the Scriptures."[11]

It must be noted that there is a difference between the illuminating work of the Holy Spirit today and revelation. Theologian and author James Rosscup explains the difference:

> Contrary to the teaching of many, neither special revelation nor inspiration are occurring today. The Bible contains God's final and complete written revelation to man (see Jude 3 and Rev. 22:18, 19). **Currently, the Holy Spirit instructs and guides a believer, not by revealing newly inspired data, but by bringing illumination to God's already revealed Word.** (emphasis added)[12]

Any time someone is declaring to have a "word from God," always make certain the word he or she heard aligns with the Scriptures and is understood in the context given.

HEART/SOUL

All references to the heart include one's mind, will, and emotions.[13] Similarly, the words *heart* and *soul* can be used interchangeably and therefore will be used as synonyms.

FAITH/BELIEVE

For the purposes of the workbook, the working definition of faith will include three facets:

1. A firm conviction of truth (God's Word)—God's Spirit using God's Word

2. The personal surrender of your will to God's will (God's Word)

3. Your obedience to God's Word

Notice all three facets center around and find their basis in the Word of God. Furthermore, all three facets must be present to have a biblical faith. For example, if a person only has a firm conviction but refuses to surrender his or her will and obey, that person merely exhibits head knowledge. Head knowledge does not save. According to James, those who hear the Word but refuse to be doers of the Word (through personal surrender of the will and obedience) are in danger of deluding themselves (James 1:22) and are no different from demons who believe and yet shudder (James 2:19). The Lord God is not impressed with man's head knowledge; rather, He is after the heart. Heart knowledge involves all three facets of faith.[14]

REPENTANCE

The word *repentance* is the Greek word *metanoia*, which means "a change of mind."[15] This change of mind is the cause of a person's change in direction. Platt, in his book *Follow Me*, explains the significance of repentance and describes its meaning:

The very first word out of Jesus' mouth in His ministry in the New Testament is clear: repent. Repentance is a rich biblical term that signifies an elemental transformation in someone's mind, heart, and life. When people repent, they turn from walking in one direction to running in the opposite direction. From that point forward, they think differently, believe differently, feel differently, love differently, and live differently.[16]

Look at 2 Timothy 2:25b–26 and answer the following questions.

1. Who grants repentance? _____

2. What will repentance lead to according to verse 25? _____

_____

3. What is the result of repentance according to verse 26?

   a. _____

   b. _____

4. According to verse 26, the one who needs to repent is being held captive by the enemy to do what?

_____

Have you ever looked at repentance in this way?

In summary, Paul is instructing Timothy about those who are in opposition to the truth. In essence, only God can grant repentance. When God grants repentance, it always leads to a knowledge of the truth, which is necessary because the person in opposition is deceived by Satan. The deception is causing an inability to think correctly, which is to think biblically. When the one who opposes the truth begins to acknowledge the truth by obedience, they will "come to their senses." This will enable them to escape from the snare or trap that the enemy has had them in—namely, deception and sin.

Did you notice that the person who is in the snare of the enemy is actually doing the will of the enemy? Whose will do you obey? For additional reading on the subject of repentance, I would highly recommend the following books:

1. *The Doctrine of Repentance*[17]

2. *Repentance: The First Word of the Gospel.*[18]

Now, after having looked at the need for discipleship and the biblical solution, as well as the terms associated with discipleship, let's get started with the actual process of discipleship. We will start at the beginning, with salvation.

NOTES

CHAPTER 3

THE BEGINNING: SALVATION

"Then he [Abraham] believed in the LORD; and He
reckoned it to him as righteousness."
(Gen. 15:6)

"But God demonstrates His own love toward us,
in that while we were yet sinners,
Christ died for us. Much more then, having now been justified by His blood,
we shall be saved from the wrath of God through Him."
(Rom. 5:8–9)

I realize that some of you may be picking up this workbook and thinking, *I thought this was a book on discipleship.* And so it is. However, I am concerned that one of the issues with discipleship within the church is based on the fact that we are working diligently to disciple the unsaved. Therefore, lest it be an assumption or too obvious, allow me reiterate the fact that we can *only* disciple those who are already His!

There is much attention being given today to the topic of salvation. There is a much-needed concern resonating from some of the leading pastors and pulpits today in regard to the "easy believism" of our day. John MacArthur, in his book *The Gospel According to Jesus*, confronts the issue head-on:

> Listen to the typical gospel presentation nowadays. You will hear sinners entreated with words like, "accept Jesus Christ as personal Savior"; "ask Jesus into your heart"; "invite Christ into your life"; or "make a decision for Christ." You may be so accustomed to hearing those phrases that it will surprise you to learn that none of them is based on biblical terminology. They are the products of a diluted gospel. It is not the gospel according to Jesus.

> The gospel Jesus proclaimed was a call to discipleship, a call to follow Him in submissive obedience, not just a plea to make a decision or pray

a prayer. Jesus' message liberated people from the bondage of their sin while it confronted and condemned hypocrisy. It was an offer of eternal life and forgiveness for repentant sinners, but at the same time it was a rebuke to outwardly religious people whose lives were devoid of true righteousness. It put sinners on notice that they must turn from sin and embrace God's righteousness. It was in every sense good news, yet it was **anything but easy-believism**. (emphasis added)[19]

Similarly, pastor and author David Platt is also sounding the alarm today, warning of the "deception that has spread like wildfire across the contemporary Christian landscape."[20] Platt questions the typical Christian clichés such as "Just ask Jesus into your heart. Simply invite Christ into your life. Repeat this prayer after me, and you will be saved."[21] He then asks, "Should it alarm us that the Bible never mentions such a prayer?"[22]

Likewise, pastor and author J.D. Greear, in his book titled *Stop Asking Jesus into Your Heart*, states, "Salvation is not a prayer you pray in a one-time ceremony and then move on from; salvation is a posture of repentance and faith that you begin in a moment and maintain for the rest of your life."[23]

As I consider the gospel message as it appears in the Scriptures and these statements from pastors and authors I trust, I cannot help but question the authenticity of salvation within the church. Likewise, as I counsel women who are basing their salvation on a prayer they prayed forty years prior with no evidence of change in their life, I cannot help but think about the warning the Lord Jesus gave in Matthew 7:13–27.

The words of Matthew 7:21–23 are probably the most sobering words in all of Scripture. As you work through the following section in the workbook, prayerfully consider and heed the warning Jesus, in His mercy, spoke. In these passages of the Sermon on the Mount, Jesus warned of the false assurance "many" would have on "that day." Look at the following passages below and in Matthew 7:21-23 and prayerfully allow the Lord to open your mind "to understand the Scriptures" (Luke 24:45).

First and foremost, salvation is from the Lord (Jonah 2:9; Ps. 3:8; Isa. 12:2; 43:11; 45:22; 45:17). It is a transaction solely within the Godhead. In fact, God's plan of salvation is beautifully outlined in the first chapter of Ephesians: the Father's plan (vv. 3–6), the Son's perfect execution of the plan (vv. 7–12), and now, the Spirit's application of the plan as He uses the Word (vv. 13–14), all to the praise of His glory (vv. 6, 12, 14).

Now, answer the following questions using Matthew 7:13–27.

1. Jesus specifically identifies two gates (ways) in Matthew 7:13–14. In the space provided list the facts regarding the two gates.

Wide Gate   Narrow Gate

Wide Gate (Broad Way)	Narrow Gate (Narrow Way)
Leads to _____	Leads to _____
_____ are those who enter by it.	_____ are those who find it.

2. Which gate are we instructed to enter according to verse 13? _____

3. Immediately after warning about the two gates, the Lord Jesus begins to warn in verse 15 about _____ _____ .

4. In verse 15, Jesus gives an external and internal description of the false prophets. How does He describe them?

External Description	Internal Description

5. What does it tell you that the false prophet can outwardly look like a sheep? In other words, what might that look like?

_____

_____

_____

6. Jude also warns the "beloved" (Jude 3) about false prophets. Look at Jude 4 and record where the false prophet is in relation to the beloved. _____

7. How did the false prophet get in? _____

8. Was he noticed when he crept in? _____ Why? In other words, think about how this could happen. What might he be doing to "fit in"?

_____

_____

9. Now let's return to Matthew 7. According to verse 15, who initiates the encounter with the false prophet? _____

10. How are we to "know" the false prophet according to verse 16? _____

11. What question does Jesus ask in verse 16 in regard to the fruit? _____

_____ ?

Think about it. Grapes and figs are fruits that you can eat. They provide nourishment and are good for you. However, thorns and thistles also come from trees. But they can provide no nourishment. In fact, they can be hurtful and they are useless.

1. In verses 17–19, Jesus gives further explanation of "fruit" by comparing two types of trees. List the facts from each.

Good Tree

Bad Tree

Good Tree	Bad Tree
Bears _____	Bears _____
Cannot produce _____	Cannot produce _____
	Cannot produce _____

It might interest you to know that the word "bear" in these verses is in the present tense. In other words, it is the habit of their lifestyle or walk.

2. In verse 20, Jesus once again tells us how the false prophet will be truly known. What does He say?

_____

3. Now let's look at the most disturbing verses of all, Matthew 7:21–23. I say this because in these verses Jesus is describing someone who is deceived. This person thinks he or she is saved and will find out, in the end, that he or she was the one deceived. These are some of the saddest verses in all of Scripture to me, personally.

a. First, what do these people call Jesus on that day? _____.

The name "Lord" is the Greek word *kurios*, which means "Master, Owner, Possessor."[24]

b. By calling Jesus this name, what are they saying about Him? _____

_____

c. What is the true characteristic of the one who calls Jesus Lord in verse 21? "He who _____ the _____ of My Father who is in heaven."

d. Look up and record the cross-reference in Luke 6:46. _____

_____

In other words, Jesus makes a clear distinction between those who merely call Him Lord and those who obey Him as the Lord. If Jesus is truly Lord of our lives, we will do what the Master says.

e. Look at Matthew 7:22 in the NASB and note the first word Jesus uses. _____

I find the word "Many" most disturbing. Isn't that how He described those on the broad way in verse 13?

f. What will the MANY say on that day to the Lord?
   Did we not: _____
   and _____
   and _____ ?

g. What are they saying? In other words, what are they pointing to or counting on?

_____

Are they not pointing to things they have done—in essence, their works? Is it possible to be "religious" and still miss Christ? Is it possible to "do" without "being"?

h. More importantly, what does Jesus say in verse 23? _____

_____

The word "knew" in verse 23 is the Greek word *ginosko*, which means "to know experientially."[25] According to John MacArthur, "'to know' was a Hebrew idiom that represented intimate relations. . . . Jesus therefore will say to those who claim Him but never trusted in Him, **I never knew you.** 'I have never known you as My disciples, and you have never known Me as your Lord and Savior. We have no intimate part of each other. You chose your kingdom, and it was not My kingdom.'"26

    i. What were those who called Jesus Lord doing according to verse 23? _____

_____.

I find it interesting that Jesus does not take into account what they say; rather, He is more concerned by what they are doing. Remember, to say one thing and do another is the definition of deception. For what we really believe is what we do.

4. And last, let's look at the verses we have heard since most of us were little children, Matthew 7:24–27. This time, Jesus will compare two types of people: the wise man and the foolish man. Let's compare the facts using verses 24–27. Please note you will need to use the NASB to fill in the blanks correctly.

Wise Man	Foolish Man
Hears God's _____	Hears God's _____
_____ upon God's Word.	Does _____ act upon God's Word.
Built house on _____.	Built house on the _____.
Rain _____.	Rain _____.
Floods _____.	Floods _____.
Winds _____ and burst against the house.	Winds _____ and burst against the house.
The house _____ because it was founded upon the rock.	The house _____ and great was its fall.

5. Looking at the facts from Matthew 7:24–27, what is the difference between the two men?

_____

_____

_____

6. Now, look at James 1:22. Record the verse. _____

_____

7. As you look at James 1:22, what is the result for the person who hears God's Word but is not a doer of the Word? _____

Is this what Jesus is warning about in Matthew 7:21-23 and 24-27? Think about it. To think you are saved and find out you are really lost—wouldn't that be the GREATEST DECEPTION OF ALL?

So what does this have to do with discipleship? The **FIRST** step when discipling others is to start at the beginning. Therefore, the first thing I have someone do when they come to be discipled is to tell me their salvation story. In others words, I invite them to share with me when they were drawn by the Spirit's power to make Jesus Christ both Lord and Savior of their lives. What about you? What is your story?

_____

_____

_____

_____

When Jesus Christ is truly the Lord and Savior of your life, there will be a change in your mind, will, and emotions. In essence, He will give you a new heart!

8. Look at Ezekiel 36:26–27 and answer the following questions:

    a. What does the Lord specifically promise to give in verse 26?

        i. A new _____

        ii. A new _____

    b. What will He put in our spirit according to verse 27? _____

    c. What will His Spirit in us **CAUSE** us to do according to verse 27? _____

Recently, I have had the joy and privilege of reading about the conversion of a woman named Rosaria Champagne Butterfield. Her incredible testimony can be found in her book titled *The Secret Thoughts of an Unlikely Convert*. Rosaria candidly describes her life before Christ:

> I was an associate professor at Syracuse University, recently tenured in the English Department also holding a joint teaching appointment in the Center for Women's Studies. I was in a lesbian relationship with a woman who was primarily an animal activist. . . We were members of a Unitarian Universalist Church, where I was the coordinator of what is called the Welcoming Committee, the gay and lesbian advocacy group.[27]

She begins her book by stating, "How do I tell you about my conversion to Christianity without making it sound like an alien abduction or a train wreck? Truth be told, it felt like a little of both."[28] She further describes what happened when she accepted Christ and Savior: "Making a commitment to Christ was not merely a philosophical shift. It was not a one-step process. It did not involve rearranging the surface prejudices and fickle loyalties of my life. Conversion did not 'fit' into my life. Conversion overhauled my soul and personality."[29]

Wow! When I read her book and specifically her personal testimony, I cannot help but see Ezekiel 36:26–27. Isn't that what our testimony should look like? Everything in Rosaria's life changed. EVERYTHING! This is not the testimony of someone who simply tried to change her behavior. Truthfully, she saw no need for a change in behavior. She was not struggling with her identity as a lesbian—that is, until she met Christ and read His Word.

This is the testimony of a woman who allowed the Lord Jesus to give her a new spirit and heart. The life changes Rosaria describes in her book are a depiction of a truly "new creation."

9. Look at 2 Corinthians 5:17 and record the verse. _____

_____

_____

WHAT ABOUT YOU?

Your testimony may not look exactly like Rosaria's, but it is still very much the same in the eyes of the Lord. Let's look at salvation from His perspective.

Look at Acts 26:18 and answer the following questions:

1. Who is going to open a person's eyes? (You will need to look in the previous verses for the answer.)

_____

2. What happens to the person whose eyes the Lord has opened? _____

Remember, the word "turn" in this verse is synonymous with the word *repent*.

3. What specifically has the person turned from?
_____ to _____

The dominion of _____ to the dominion of _____

4. Why? In other words, what is the purpose of turning from these things? What will they receive?

_____

_____

Don't you think that a person who turns from the darkness to the light, from the dominion of Satan to the dominion of God, should demonstrate evidence of these truths?

Therefore, since Jesus has become the Lord/Master of your life, what changes have you noticed? In other words, has there been a transformation or evidence of His fruit? List some of the things that you have seen as evidence that He truly is the Lord and Savior of your life.

_____

_____

_____

_____

A PERSONAL EXAMPLE

The Lord never ceases to amaze me. While writing this chapter, a woman, who I will refer to as Denise, was asking to be discipled. As always, we began the discipleship process with her salvation. As I began to write down the things she said, I could hardly believe what I was hearing. The timing of this encounter could not have been more confirming. The following is the conversation that ensued.

Mendy: So, Denise, let's begin with you telling me about your salvation. Denise: I know that I am saved.

Mendy: Okay. Upon what are you basing your salvation? Denise: (After a long pause)

I pray.

I read my Bible.

I study my Bible.

I love my family.

I try to be a good example at work.

I am in a helping profession, so I try to help the people I see.

I can recognize that the good things in my life come from the hand of God.

Just going to church—because if I did what I wanted to do, I would stay home. I go because I am supposed to go.

[As I heard the list of deeds Denise was performing, my heart began to sink. I realized quickly that Denise was basing her salvation on works. It troubled me greatly because the one thing I kept hearing was the word "I," and the only missing factor was Jesus Christ or the cross. She never said one word about the Lord. So I continued to probe, thinking maybe she did not understand my question.]

Mendy: So can you tell me about when you were saved? How old were you? Can you tell me any of the details?

Denise: Oh yes. I was seven years old. I remember my mom told me that I was asking a lot of questions. I do not remember the questions I was asking, though. My mom set up an appointment with my pastor. I remember sitting in his office. He talked to me. I'm really not sure what he said, though. I don't remember much about it. I do remember it was on a Wednesday afternoon, because that evening I went forward after the message. That's when I was saved.

Mendy: So when you went forward, why did you go?

Denise: I do not really know. I just thought it was time to become a Christian.

Mendy: So when you went forward, did you pray a prayer or did you cry out to the Lord to save you?

Denise: No. I didn't say or do anything. I just went forward. I was baptized a couple of months later . . . I think.

Mendy: When you went forward, did you sense anything had happened or notice any change in your life afterward?

Denise: Well . . . (pause) . . . No.

Mendy: Have you ever felt the weight and heaviness of your sin?

Denise: (After a long pause) Well, no. I can say I have never felt the weight of my sin.

[At this point in the meeting, I am having significant doubts and am pretty sure Denise does not have a personal relationship with the Lord.]

Denise: Oh yeah, and one more thing. When I was eighteen years old, I heard a preacher that was talking about rededication and doubts about salvation. I remember thinking about my salvation and having some doubts, but then I remembered that I was saved because of what happened to me when I was seven years old. (She paused.) But then again, what does a seven-year-old know?

Mendy: Denise, may I share with you my testimony? I was six years old when I was saved.

Denise: Sure.

Mendy: I remember very clearly the day I was saved. I can actually replay the scene in my head. I was attending Vacation Bible School at our church. We had heard about Jesus all week. It was on a Thursday morning, and the woman who was sharing the gospel was doing a chalk drawing of the cross while she told about the death of Christ as He took on my sin. I remember I could hardly believe what I was hearing. I distinctly remember being drawn to the love of the One on that cross. I could hardly believe He would die for me. I felt dirty and knew somehow that He died for me. I know now that what I was experiencing was the conviction of the Holy Spirit. I did not know it then, nor could I have put it into words, but I know now that the Holy Spirit was drawing me. I could hardly wait until the teacher finished so that I could go forward and ask Jesus to come into my heart and save me. I remember almost running down that aisle. But what I remember most is that I was running to Him! I cried out to the Lord and asked Him to save me and come and live in my heart. I also remember when I got home telling my mother that I felt so clean inside. She affirmed what I was saying and told me that was very normal. From that day on, I have had a love for Jesus that has never left me. Even though I was never discipled and have many regrets, I was never the same after that day. Since I asked Jesus into my heart, I have always loved Jesus and wanted to please Him. When I did sin, and still do sin, I am grieved in my heart because I want to live to please and honor Him.

Denise: Wow!

Mendy: Denise, I am not saying that your experience is not valid because your experience is not like mine. But, did you hear a difference? What am I basing my salvation upon?

Denise: Jesus . . . the cross.

Mendy: Yes! (Sensing the Holy Spirit leading me to take her to Matthew 7:21–23, I continued.) Now, I want to take you to a passage of Scripture where the Lord speaks about this issue. Denise: Okay.

Mendy: Turn to Matthew 7:21–23.

As Denise read the passages, she paused with tears streaming down her face like a fountain. She apologized for crying. I told her there was no need to apologize. I read her back the list she gave me when I asked her what she was basing her salvation upon. I then asked her if she thought it sounded like the people in Matthew 7:21–22. She said, "Yes, it does." I asked her to reread the Lord's response in Matthew 7:23. As she read it, she wept. She then told me she felt like she needed to go home so that she could think about all that had been said. I began praying that the Holy Spirit would draw Denise to the Lord Jesus and His cross, and that He would grant her "repentance leading to the knowledge of the truth," so that she could "come to [her] senses and escape from the snare of the devil" (2 Tim. 2:25b–26).

The conversation recorded above occurred on a Thursday afternoon at my house. I am overwhelmed with great joy and awe at our Savior and Lord to report that three days later, in a prayer meeting at my church, Denise went forward to receive Christ. I cannot even begin to express the gratitude I had to the Lord as I heard her cry out to the Lord Jesus for forgiveness as she asked Him to be the Lord and Savior of her life. I wish I could adequately describe the change in her countenance afterward. If I had to try to put it into words, I would say I saw relief, peace, and great joy!

What is even more telling is the text I received from her a couple of days after she cried out to the Lord. She described a new desire to be in His Word and the ability to actually understand what it says. When I asked her what the Lord had been showing her from His Word, she stated, "Well, I know that He loves me!" Her countenance and smile told me that now she actually believed Him. I have also noticed that Denise has a strong desire to know His Word and do His will.

One of the biggest things I have noticed has been a change in her heart in regard to her parents. When I initially met Denise, she was filled with hatred and disgust toward her parents. She blamed all her depression, anxiety, and fear on them. She had been to numerous counselors (some of whom were Christians) who only helped her solidify her hatred and blame.

Since her conversion, the Lord has revealed to her that she needs to ask her parents for forgiveness for the hatred, anger, and bitterness she has felt against them for many years. She has not spoken to her parents for seven years. She is in the process of contacting them to ask for their forgiveness! Only the Lord God can cause this type of heart change!

For He—and only He—has "delivered us from the domain of darkness, and transferred us to the kingdom of His beloved Son" (Col. 1:13). The evidence that this has happened to Denise is being walked out in her everyday life. In essence, her life is changing! Praise You, Lord Jesus, for drawing Denise and saving her in Your infinite mercy and grace! What a Savior! As you read Denise's story, you may be saying to yourself, "That sounds a lot like my story." You may be wondering what it truly means to be saved. Prayerfully consider the following information.

WHAT DOES IT MEAN TO BE SAVED?

The word *salvation* is derived from the Greek word *soteria*, which denotes deliverance and preservation.[30] Salvation is viewed in three tenses: past, present, and future. Or more specifically, justification, sanctification, and glorification, respectively.

First, remember salvation is entirely a work of God.

Look at the following passages and record the verses or missing words.

1. John 6:44– _____

_____

2. 1 Peter 1:3–"Blessed be the God and Father of our Lord Jesus Christ, who according to His great mercy _____ us to be born again to a living hope through the resurrection of Jesus Christ from the dead."

Did you see it? Who is the "cause"? _____

3. James 1:18– _____

_____

_____

   a. Whose will is being exercised in this verse? _____

   b. How does He bring us forth? _____

As the Lord God draws you to Himself by the power of His Spirit, the invitation is extended for you to come in faith to receive what you need most—a Savior. Yes, you must be saved out of darkness and Satan's dominion into the kingdom of light and under the lordship and dominion of Jesus Christ. That is what happens when He justifies you. He saves you from sin's **penalty**, which is death (Rom. 6:23).

However, lest we think salvation has only one tense—the past—we may not realize or we may forget that we need a Savior on a daily basis. This is what sanctification is all about. Jesus Christ is still saving you. He is saving you from the **power** of sin so that you might walk in the newness of life He has granted (Rom. 6:4) as you surrender your will and walk in obedience to His Word.

Jesus said, "I came that they might have life, and might have it abundantly" (John 10:10). But as I look around the church, I do not see an overwhelming amount of abundant life. What does it mean to have abundant life? What will that look like? To answer these questions, we must first lay a foundation in terms of salvation and its three tenses. Consider the following chart to help you understand the meaning of the three tenses involved in salvation.[31]

The Three Tenses of Salvation		
Tense	Theological Term	What's Happening to Me
Past	**Justification**—This happens in a moment in time when the Father draws us to the Lord Jesus by His Spirit and His Word and we respond in faith. The word *justification* means to "declare righteous."[32]	"I *have been saved* from the **PENALTY** of sin."
Present	**Sanctification**—This is a process that occurs the moment a person is saved and continues until death. Sanctification is a progressive work of God whereby God's Spirit uses the Word to conform the believer more and more to the image of Christ as we surrender our will and obey His Word.	"I *am being saved* from the **POWER** of sin."
Future	**Glorification**—This is the future and final state of the believer. Glorification refers to the time when, at the Second Coming, those who have died in Christ—along with all living believers—will be given resurrected bodies.[34]	"I *will be saved* from the **PRESENCE** of sin."

As you consider the chart on the previous page, prayerfully ask the Lord where you are in regard to your relationship with Him. You may also want to consider the following verses of Scripture and answer the subsequent questions for help.

1. Look at 2 Corinthians 13:5. Notice that Paul is exhorting *the church* in Corinth.

    a. What is Paul urging the church in Corinth to do? _____

b. What should they be able to recognize about themselves? _____

_____

_____

c. What did Paul warn in this verse? _____

Note: I find it interesting that Paul is exhorting those in the church of Corinth to test themselves. Could it be that not everyone who professes Christ actually possesses Christ? This is not a test you want to fail!

2. Look at Psalm 139:23 and record the verse. _____

_____

_____

_____

Now, pray this verse back to the Lord and listen for His answer.

Salvation will always begin with God, who graciously reveals our sin and need for a Savior, and it ends with the provision of His Son on the cross. And yet, salvation will also reveal the need for a daily Savior as we walk and grow in Him through obedience to His Word. The necessity of discipleship is vital, but it hinges on this truth! If the Lord, in His mercy, reveals to your heart that you are not His, then "turn to [Jesus Christ], and be saved" (Isa. 45:22). If you go to another person, make sure they take you to the Word of God and point you to the Savior, where you can see the truth. Please do not proceed if there is any doubt.

NOTES

CHAPTER 4

A BIBLICAL MODEL FOR DISCIPLESHIP

"I am writing to you, little children, because your
sins are forgiven you for His name's sake.

I am writing to you, fathers, because you know
Him who has been from the beginning.

I am writing to you, young men, because you have overcome the evil
one. I have written to you, children, because you know the Father.

I have written to you, fathers, because you know
Him who has been from the beginning.

I have written to you, young men, because you are strong, and the
word of God abides in you, and you have overcome the evil one."

(1 John 2:12–14)

THE DIAGNOSTIC TOOL OF 1 JOHN 2:12–14

Any physician knows that making a correct diagnosis begins with possessing accurate diagnostic tools. A visit to the doctor normally results in various tests, including a physical examination, blood tests, and vital signs. If our evaluation does not fall within the normal-range category, further tests are needed until optimal heath is achieved.

Likewise, and even more importantly, we should assess our spiritual condition regularly (2 Cor. 13:5). With the goal of spiritual maturation in mind, we need an accurate tool to help in the diagnosis. The biblical mandate is clear. Jesus instructed His disciples, "Make disciples . . . [by] teaching them to observe all that I commanded you" (Matt. 28:19–20). If we are going to make disciples, we must be able to determine accurately where the disciple is in the process and what is needed for growth. Therefore, we cannot overestimate the necessity of an accurate diagnostic tool—God's Word.

With the goal of spiritual maturity in mind, Paul clearly stated, "And we proclaim Him, admonishing every man and teaching every man with all wisdom, that we may present every man complete in Christ. And for this purpose also I labor, striving according to His power, which mightily works within me" (Col. 1:28–29). These words should be the mandate for every discipleship leader who teaches with the goal of spiritual maturation in mind. You might ask, "Where does the process begin?" and "Does the Bible offer a guide or diagnostic tool toward spiritual maturity?" The answer to both of these questions is in 1 John 2:12–14. Before we begin to observe the text, we must place 1 John 2:12–14 in context. Context always rules the interpretation of a passage!

First John is a letter (epistle) written by the apostle John to believers sometime between AD 85 and John states the purpose of the letter as "These things I have written *to you who believe* in the name of the Son of God, in order that you may know that you have eternal life" (1 John 5:13, emphasis added). Therefore, this is a letter written to believers.

The believers who are addressed in John's first epistle are in need of encouragement and assurance. Amid external persecution and turmoil, false teachers are beginning to infiltrate the church, causing division and uncertainty. Whether internal or external, persecution always has a way of exposing those who profess Christ but do not possess Christ. Therefore, those who are not genuinely born from above have left the church (1 John 2:19). John approaches the situation as a pastor who guards, guides, and grazes his flock. Specifically, in 1 John 2:12–14, the apostle John addresses the subject of spiritual maturity. To make an accurate assessment of where you are spiritually, you must first consider this Scripture.

OBSERVING 1 JOHN 2:12–14

Let's begin by observing and recording the facts.

1. Looking at 1 John 2:12, what fact do you see about the "little children"?

---

* It may interest you to know that the term "little children" is the Greek word *teknion*, which is used figuratively as a term of affection by a teacher to his disciples.[35] The Greek word *teknion* is used throughout the entire book of 1 John; however, in 1 John 2:13 and 18, the Greek word *paidion* is used, which means "a very young child, infant, used of boys and girls; of a newborn child."[36]

2. Why do you think John uses an entirely different Greek word in these passages?

_____

_____

The difference in use of terms is worth noting in regard to interpretation of the text and in order to differentiate the three distinct levels of spiritual maturity. In the next two verses, he will categorize his "little children" or pupils into three levels of spiritual maturity. Let's look at the three levels and the facts regarding each group.

3. Look at 1 John 2:13. What are the three distinct levels of spiritual maturity addressed as you consider the following illustrations?

   a. _____

   b. _____

   c. _____

4. Now let's take each group and list the facts concerning each group as they appear in Scripture.

    a. **Fathers/Mothers** – _____ (1 John 2:13–14).

    b. **Young Men/Women** –   1) _____

                                 2) _____

                                 3) _____

(1 John 2:13–14).

    c. **Children/Baby** (*paidion*) – _____ (1 John 2:13).

Remember, the word "children" in 1 John 2:13 is the Greek word *paidion*, which means immature one or baby.

If you were to structure 1 John 2:12–14, it would look like this:

v. 12 I am writing to little children (*teknion*)

$\downarrow$

because your sins are forgiven you

$\downarrow$

for His name's sake

v. 13 I am writing to you **fathers**

I have written $\downarrow$

because you know Him

$\downarrow$

who has been from the beginning

vv. 13–14 I am writing to you **young men**

I have written $\downarrow$

because you have overcome the evil one
you are strong
the Word of God abides in you

v. 13   I have written to you **children** (*paidion*)

$\downarrow$

because you know the Father

As we attempt to interpret the meaning of the text, you will recall, as previously defined, the word "know," which is the Greek word *ginosko*. This word denotes personal fellowship with God or Christ and also between the Father and the Son. In other words, since the Father and the Son know each other, they love one another (John 3:35). The same relationship exists between the Lord Jesus and His disciples (John 13:1).[37] Therefore, this term describes knowledge that is experiential, personal, and relational. [38]

Through a casual observation of the text, it would appear as if the spiritual fathers and the children have the same characteristic. They each have some knowledge of God; however, common sense tells us this cannot be true. The key to correct interpretation lies in the subjects: the terms "children" and "fathers."

5. Considering the definition of the word "know" and the distinct terms for the subjects used, answer the following questions.

    a. What does a little baby know about his earthly father? _____

    _____

    b. What do you think a spiritual baby would know about his heavenly Father?

    _____

    c. What do you think a spiritual father would know about his heavenly Father?

    _____

    d. Is the knowledge of the spiritual baby the same as the knowledge of the spiritual father in relation to our heavenly Father? Explain your answer.

    _____

    _____

    _____

Can you see that the spiritual father's personal, relational, and experiential knowledge is vastly greater than the knowledge of a spiritual baby?

6. Now let's consider the young men and compare them with the children.

    a. Do you believe that the three specific characteristics listed about the young men are also true of the children? Yes   No

    b. Let's consider the opposite characteristics:

        1) Instead of being strong, the children would be considered _____ .

        2) Instead of overcoming the enemy, the children would more likely be labeled as _____ by the evil one.

        3) Instead of the Word abiding in them, the children would _____ .

7. Now, let's focus on the phrase "the word of God abides in you" (1 John 2:14). Think about it. What does it mean when the Word of God abides within us?

_____

_____

8. Notice, it does not say that the young men merely "abide in the Word." Is there a difference between the "Word abiding within" and "abiding in the Word"? Any thoughts?

_____

_____

_____

As you contemplate the difference, look at the order of the words within the text. For example, if you think about it, isn't it possible for someone to abide in the Word without having the Word of God abide within? For instance, we can all think of someone who demonstrates little to no change in their life although they faithfully attend numerous Bible studies. However, can you think of even one person with whom the Word abides who does not have a radically different life? The difference in the two phrases is the difference between information and transformation! Once again, faith is the key! When the Word of God abides within me, I am surrendering my will to God's Word and walking in obedience—and this is what makes it TRANSFORMATIONAL! Which would you rather be: informed or transformed?

I realize that for transformation to occur, you must first know what the Scripture says; therefore, information is vital. However, it is not designed to be the end result. Scripture declares, "Knowledge makes arrogant" (1 Cor. 8:1).

9. Now, let's consider those same facts about the young men and compare them with the spiritual father. Do you think that a spiritual father has the same characteristics as the young men?

Explain your answer. _____

_____

Next, let's consider the specific words used to describe the spiritual levels. John describes spiritual babies, young men, and spiritual fathers. Why did John use the term "father?" Why didn't he use the terms _spiritual babies, young men,_ and _old men_? To help answer this question, consider the following questions:

10. What does the term "fathers" imply? In other words, what must be true to be called a father?

_____

11. Who is the One who gives children? _____

12. Because the Father entrusts parents with children in the physical realm, do you think He might do so in the spiritual realm?

_____

Notice that John, under the inspiration of the Holy Spirit, chose a reproductive term. Since God is the Author of reproduction, could it be possible that discipleship in the church is not effective because spiritual babies and young men are allowed to disciple others? Does the discipleship in your church have spiritual babies trying to disciple spiritual babies? Would we allow this in the physical realm? Would we really consider putting a two-year-old in charge of the nursery? Would we consider placing a teenager in charge of other teenagers? Think about the home. If we want our children to mature in the Lord and become young men/ women and spiritual fathers/mothers, should we not be the example?

One last question to consider. Is spiritual maturation gender-specific? In other words, is it just for the male gender, OR might it also be interpreted as little children, young women, and spiritual mothers? I realize the Scriptures particularly target the men because they are designed by God to be the spiritual leaders in the home and church. However, women need to grow in Christ so they can disciple children (especially their own) and other women. Now that we have observed the three levels of spiritual maturity found in 1 John 2:12–14, consider the following interpretation.[39]

INTERPRETING 1 JOHN 2:12–14

The apostle John is writing to his "children" in the faith. The term he uses to describe his "children" (*teknion*) throughout the letter is the equivalent of a teacher to his pupils, with the exception of two places—namely, 1 John 2:13 and 18. He states in the first part of 1 John 2:12, "I am writing to you, little children." Since he is writing as a teacher to his pupils, John is including all believers in the statement. We know this because of what follows: "because your sins are forgiven you for His name's sake."

However, in 1 John 2:13, John will begin to differentiate the believers he is addressing by categorizing them into three distinct groups: little children (*paidion*), young men, and fathers. At first glance, the facts concerning the little children and the fathers seem identical. But when you consider the label each is given, there is a marked difference. For example, the word "know" literally means to know by experience. Consider the following question: "How well does a little baby know his parent?" The obvious answer is very little. The baby may be able to recognize a distinguishing voice, face, or even smell, but he will have very little capability for knowing anything beyond this basic information. Therefore, when thinking in spiritual terms, the spiritual baby has very little experiential knowledge about the Lord. The father, on the other hand, has the capability of knowing by experience so much more about the Lord, having walked with Him for a much longer time.

Likewise, when you look at the facts concerning the young man, you will see that he is strong, that he is able to overcome the evil one, and that the Word of God abides in him. As you begin to compare the spiritual baby with the young man, you can deduce that what is true of the young man is not true of the spiritual baby, since these facts are not stated in regard to the spiritually immature. In other words, the spiritual baby, more than likely, could be described as being weak and overcome by the enemy (at least in some areas of life), and the Word of God is not abiding as consistently within him, in comparison to the young man.

Similarly, the spiritual father, in comparison to the young man, is very strong and is able to consistently overcome the evil one because the Word of God abides within him as a way of life. In fact, because John chose to use a reproductive term when he chose the word "father," the spiritual father is mature enough to help disciple others in this maturation process called sanctification.

APPLYING 1 JOHN 2:12–14

What About You?

Prayerfully ask the Holy Spirit to lead you to the truth concerning your spiritual level of maturity. Consider the following chart as you pray. In what areas are you spiritually weak? In what ways/areas may the enemy be overcoming you? Be honest before the Lord and remember: "All things are open and laid bare" before Him (Heb. 4:13).

SPIRITUAL LEVELS OF MATURITY
1 John 2:12–14

**"I am writing to you, little children, because your sins
are forgiven you for His name's sake."**
(1 John 2:12)

Teknion ~ Teacher to Pupil

Fathers/Mothers	Young Men/Women	Children *Paidion* (Immature One/ Baby)
1 John 2:13–14 *You know Him who has been from thebeginning.	1 John 2:13–14 *You have overcome the evil one. *You are strong. *The Word of God abides in you.	1 John 2:13–14 *You know the Father.
Interpretation You are consistently over-coming the evil one.You are strong. The Word of God abides in you consistently.These characteristics have been evident in your life for some time. The reproductive terminol-ogy used implies that the Lord has blessed you with spiritual children. You are equipped and ready to teach spiritual babies and the young men/women how to grow in each of these aspects of truth.	Interpretation You have qualities/fruit that display spiritual maturity, and you are growing in them consistently. You are continuing to grow and in God's timing are in the process of becoming a spiritual father/mother.	Interpretation Your knowledge of the Lord is like that of an infant or a child to his parent. You are not consistently able to overcome the evil one. More than likely, you are being overcome more frequently than you like. You are spiritually weak. The Word of God does not abide within you on a consistent basis because you do not know it or you are not consistent in your obedience to God's Word.

In conclusion, spiritual weakness and an inability to overcome the enemy are distinguish-ing marks of a spiritual baby. This can be the result of ignorance of God's Word and/or a heart that refuses to surrender the will and obey the truth of God's Word. In other words, the Word of God does not abide within you consistently. This was true in my life. Sadly, I was a spiritual baby for years (twenty-five, to be exact) because of an ignorance of God's Word. I discovered that the remedy for ignorance is Bible study. Not the kind of Bible study that merely gives you information, but one that will help you in regard to transformation. However, if you have been exposed to clear instruction from God's Word and yet have chosen to rebel against it, you are spiritually weak and have opened yourself up to being overcome by the evil one. Every time we choose not to obey God's Word, an exchange takes place in our hearts (minds, wills, and emotions). We exchange the truth of God for a lie, and our hearts become deceived and are hardened to some degree. The levels of deception and hardness are indicative of the level of truth we have received and rejected. If the Holy Spirit has shown you from His Word that you are a spiritual baby, the following chapters will provide biblical guidance necessary for you to grow. In the next chapter, we will lay some foundational truths necessary for discipleship and spiritual growth in regard to truth, deception, and the heart of man.

CHAPTER 5

HOW TO OVERCOME THE EVIL ONE

PART ONE: ESTABLISHING THE BIBLICAL FRAMEWORK USING GENESIS 3

THE VOICES IN MY HEAD

"My sheep hear My *voice*, and I know them, and they follow Me."
(John 10:27 emphasis added)

As I sat across the table from this soft-spoken and gentle young woman, no one would have suspected that there was a very serious problem. Just hours before, in a telephone conversation, Karen had revealed her desperate need for help. The frequent panic attacks had left her unable to drive a car for the past two years. I listened as Karen described the thoughts in her head that were literally paralyzing her. The counseling appointment had to be scheduled around her husband's work schedule, so that he could drive her and take care of their two-year-old son. With tears streaming down her face, Karen confessed the guilt she carried in regard to her son. She described how he spent his days sitting in front of the television for hours, eating whatever was easiest to open.

She confessed that even bathing him was an irregular occurrence.

Similarly, Karen explained that her home was in utter chaos because of her depression as the laundry piled up and the dishes were left unattended for days on end. When asked what she did throughout the day, Karen hung her head and confessed that her days were spent with countless hours in front of the television and late nights on Facebook and Pinterest. She blamed her inability to sleep on the thoughts that controlled her mind and expressed frustration because she could not seem to shut them out.

Questions about her relationship with her husband brought even more tears as she described a kind man who was getting weary of the responsibility of having a "sick" wife. Outwardly, her demeanor seemed calm and controlled; however, inwardly there was a war raging in her mind that was anything but peaceful.

As I inquired about her relationship with the Lord, she admitted it was almost nonexistent. Karen explained that at the age of fifteen, she had heard the gospel and "asked Jesus to come into her life" to save her. However, since that time, Karen admitted that there had been little to no lasting change as a result. After I inquired about what she knew concerning the fall of mankind, she struggled to biblically explain man's need for a Savior, and I sensed the Holy Spirit directing me to take her to Genesis 3.

As Karen began to read aloud, "Now the serpent was more crafty than any beast of the field which the LORD God had made. And **he said to the woman** . . ." (Gen 3:1, emphasis added), I sensed the Holy Spirit bringing to my mind the thought **And he is still speaking to her**. As the Spirit of God used the Word of God to speak, I confess I did not hear another word Karen read. My mind was captivated by what the Spirit of God had just illuminated to my mind about the real issue. The thought that the enemy was speaking, quite honestly, was a new thought. Oftentimes, we attribute the enemy's thoughts to our own thoughts because we do not know that the enemy is still speaking today. Any thought that does not align with the truth of God's Word, and in actuality is the antithesis of the Word of God, can be attributed to another voice—the enemy of our souls.

As I combined the illumination of this verse with the definition of the heart/soul, I sensed the Holy Spirit had wanted me to see the real root of Karen's problem—she was listening to the wrong voice. From that encounter on, the Holy Spirit began to illuminate Genesis 3 from the perspective of one's heart—namely, one's mind, will, and emotions. I began to see that the biblical foundation for discipleship / biblical counseling is found in Genesis 3. The following chapter will explain what the Spirit of truth showed me in the Word in the days that ensued.

One thing I have learned for certain: the Spirit of truth is most definitely the "spirit of counsel" (Isa. 11:2).

OVERCOMING THE EVIL ONE
EXAMINING THE HEART FROM GENESIS 3
Part One: The Mind

We will never reach spiritual maturity until we understand and recognize how to overcome the evil one on a consistent basis. The spiritual baby is weak and unable to overcome the evil one (1 John 2:12–14). In fact, the enemy is more than likely overcoming the spiritual baby. How and why is this happening? To answer these questions, we must look intently at the heart of mankind and examine the fall of man, as it is explained in Genesis 3.

We must also have a biblical definition of the word *heart*. Interestingly, the word *heart* can also be used as a synonym for one's soul. The biblical definition of one's heart/soul is vital and must be understood especially when one recognizes that the target of the enemy is the **mind**. As we examine the definition of the heart/soul, we need to note there are three components that make up the heart/soul: mind, will, and emotions.

Look at it this way:

Equally important is the order in which the three components of your spiritual heart function. For example, if you are thinking biblically, or God's thoughts, it will affect what you do and how you feel.

Invariably, women, who are being overcome by the enemy, present with their emotions leading the way. Their spiritual heart looks like this:

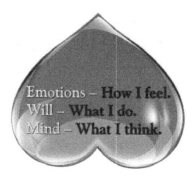

In other words, their emotions are in charge of their hearts and are directing every action and thought. When this is occurring, the enemy has succeeded in misleading their hearts.

Therefore, it is vitally important to examine what you think. Scripture states, "As [a man] thinks within himself, so he is" (Prov. 23:7). If the enemy can cause you to think incorrectly or, better still, unbiblically, you, in turn, will respond in sin, which will leave you with the emotional baggage of fear, guilt, anger, and shame.

This is what happened in the garden. Let's examine what happened in the minds, wills, and emotions of mankind by examining Genesis 3. First, we must look at what God clearly said to Adam in Genesis 2:16–17. However, God's voice was not the only voice in the garden. For the purpose of clarification, I am labeling what God said as "His" voice while attributing the enemy's words to "his" voice (emphasis on capitalization).

GOD'S VOICE

First, let's record what the Lord God said.

1. Look at Genesis 2:16–17 and list **exactly** what the Lord said to Adam.

   a. From _____ tree of the garden you may eat _____

   BUT . . .

   b. From the tree of the _____ of _____ and
      _____ you shall _____ eat.

   c. You shall surely _____ !

2. Now, let's examine the significance of what the Lord God said.

   To understand the Lord's instruction, we have to explore the reason for the stipulation placed specifically on the tree of the knowledge of good and evil.

   Why this tree?

   What was significant about it?

   What was God withholding from man?

To answer these questions, we must understand the meaning of the word "knowledge." The word "knowledge" is the Hebrew word *da at*, which by definition includes an experiential knowledge that involves relationship rather than a mere intellectual assent. Bible scholars agree: "The Hebrew was primarily concerned with life in its dynamic process, and therefore conceived knowledge as an entry into relationship with the experienced world which makes demands not only on man's understanding but also on man's will."[40]

Now reason the Scripture with me. Did man have an experiential knowledge of good? To answer this question, let's examine the following passages from Genesis 1.

a. Look at the end of the following verses and note the key repeated phrase: Genesis 1:10, 12, 18, 21, and 25.

And God saw that it was _____.

b. Now, look at God's final evaluation of all He had created in Genesis 1:31. What did He say?

And God saw all that He had made, and behold, it was _____.

c. Here's one last thought on the topic of man's knowledge concerning what was considered "good." But to gain insight concerning the word *good*, let's consider how Jesus described the term in Mark 10:17–18. What do you see? In other words, how does Jesus define *good*? _____

d. Now, look at Genesis 3:8. What is the very essence of "good" doing in this verse?

Do you see that God alone is *good*? In essence, He is the Source. Therefore, the very essence of *good* was with Adam and Eve in Genesis 3:8. Do you see it? Does it get any better than that? In fact, the LORD God was "walking in the garden in the cool of the day" to fellowship with Adam and Eve. Gloriously good! Clearly from Scripture, Adam and Eve had a unique knowledge of good, for all God had created was considered by Him "very good," as well as the personal and intimate fellowship they enjoyed with the LORD God.

3. Since we know they had a clear knowledge of good, we must ask then, "What did they NOT have experiential knowledge of in regard to the tree of the knowledge of good and evil?"

4. Now reason the Scripture with me: What was God withholding from man?

Have you ever thought of the instruction of the Lord in that way?

God, the one who gives life, the one who is rich in mercy, was instructing them not to eat from the tree that would cause them to experience the knowledge of evil, which, in turn, would lead to both their spiritual and physical deaths.

WHAT ABOUT YOU?

1. Can you relate to this? Have you ever instructed someone NOT to do something, knowing it would bring great harm to them in the end?
Describe such a situation. _____

2. In warning this individual, what were you exercising on their behalf? _____

_____

_____

3. How does the LORD God's instruction align with His character and attributes?

_____

_____

Now, let's take some time to consider the **other voice** that was in the garden.

4. Read Genesis 3:1. What do you learn about the serpent according to verse 1?

   a. What adjective does the Scripture use to describe the serpent? _____

   What does that description bring to mind? _____

   b. What is he specifically doing in verse 1? _____

   Let's record specifically what the serpent said.

5. Look at Genesis 3:1, 4–5 and list **exactly** what the serpent said to the woman.

   a. Indeed, has God said, "You shall _____ eat from _____ tree of the garden"? (Gen. 3:1).

   b. You surely shall _____ _____!

   c. God knows that in the day you eat from it your _____ will be opened, and you will _____ _____ _____, knowing _____ and _____.

Now, let's examine the significance of what the serpent said.

6. First, let's explore what the enemy said specifically in regard to God.

   a. Indeed, _____? (Gen. 3:1).

   b. God _____ that in the day you eat from it your eyes will be opened, and you will _____ _____ (Gen. 3:5).

   To understand how to overcome the enemy, you must first identify his tactics: First, the enemy will place doubt on God's Word (Gen. 3:1). Second, the enemy will place doubt on God's character (Gen. 3:5). Do you see how he questioned God's specific word and His goodness?

   c. What does it mean to doubt? _____

_____

_____

Doubt is the antithesis of faith. By definition, we have learned that faith has three components:

    1) Firm conviction of God's Word

    2) Personal surrender of the will

    3) Obedience

Using this definition, what does it mean to "doubt" God's Word and His character?

_____

_____

    Note: This is the enemy's strategy for you and me!

7. Lastly, I want you to compare the two voices in the garden. Look intently at what God said and then compare it with what the enemy said. Be specific.

    What do you see? _____

_____

_____

_____

Did you see that the enemy said the exact opposite of what God had said? Now, do you see why and how the enemy uses his voice to cause you to doubt God's voice? What about the character of God?

WHAT ABOUT YOU?

1. What has the enemy been saying to you lately that stands in direct opposition to what God would say to you in His Word?

_____

_____

2. What has the enemy been saying about the character of God that is contrary to the Word of God?

_____

_____

Now let's examine the last voice in the garden: Eve.

3. In Genesis 3:2, Eve is speaking as well. Let's examine what she is saying and to whom she is speaking.

    a. With whom is she conversing? _____

Before we go any further, do you see problem #1?

PROBLEM #1—SHE ENGAGES IN CONVERSATION WITH THE SERPENT.

Consider the following discipleship encounter.

WHITNEY'S STORY

My discipleship experience with Whitney is one I will never forget. I will always remember the day she told me about the loss of her three-year-old son and the lingering thoughts that plagued her mind daily, even six years after his death. She began to describe how she would be doing okay for a few months but then would have days when she would literally put herself to bed. She felt immense guilt for going to bed for days at a time because she had three other children and a husband at home who still needed their mother and wife. She recalled with a smile as she said, "I do not know what I would do without my husband. He allows me to go to bed and keeps the kids from bothering me. He knows I need this time, and he is so sweet to give it to me." When I asked her how often this occurred, she said, "Every few months."

Although I do not know what it is like to lose a child, I do understand the pain incurred at the loss of a child you love deeply as one of your own. My precious nephew, Matthew, died in a car wreck when he was only ten years and ten days old.

He, his twin, Katelyn, and my brother-in-law were traveling home one evening after our entire family had met to watch my son play the last ballgame of his senior year. The game was out of town. My sister had organized the entire gathering. She was not in the car because she worked a shift every three months in the CICU in the town where the ballgame was being played.

Greg had just dropped her off, made a quick run through Wendy's to get the twins their favorite ice cream, and was headed home when a deer came out from nowhere. Greg swerved to miss the deer and the car rolled several times, finally landing on its wheels.

We found out later that Matthew had been ejected. Katelyn was life-flighted to Arkansas Children's Hospital. Matthew had not survived.

I remember when my husband called to tell me that Matthew had died. He had gotten in his car and was traveling to get my sister, Dana. My daughter and I went immediately to the hospital because my sister wanted me to be there to receive and assess the twins when they arrived. At least that was the plan. In the

first call I received from my husband, as he was coming upon the scene, he said, "Mendy, there are about twelve emergency vehicles everywhere. This is a bad wreck." Five minutes later, I received the most devastating call I have ever received. My husband was crying heavily on the phone and said, "Mendy, Matthew is dead." I am not sure what happened next, but weeks later my daughter said I collapsed and was helped inside the hospital by the security guards.

I remember after the initial shock dissipated enough for me to think while in the emergency room, awaiting Katelyn and Greg, the first thoughts in my mind were NOT from the Lord. They were coming as rapid as a machine gun, one after another: *How could God allow this to happen? Ten-year-olds aren't supposed to die. Where was God? Does He not love us? What sin could we have committed that would allow this to happen? Why did God let this happen? He could have stopped it . . .* As I look back, every thought I had involved doubting God's Word and was an attack on His character.

I remember placing my hands on my head and saying out loud in the ER hallway, "Oh God, what do I know about You?" You would think after having taught the Bible for six hours that day, I could have remembered something. I could not. And as clear as if He had spoken audibly, the words came to my mind: "I am good." My initial thought was *GOOD? It doesn't feel like You are good.*

Immediately these words came to mind: You have a choice. You can believe the voices that align with how you feel or you can believe My Word." I remember saying out loud, "Lord, help me believe Your Word. Help us to give You glory in this tragic time. You will have to do it in and for us because we can't. This is too much!"

The next few hours, days, weeks, and months were a blur. I can tell you when death entered our family that Friday at 11:30 p.m. on November 2, 2007, our lives would never be the same. But at pivotal moments throughout the next several months, the Lord was near, and He was speaking as He brought Scripture to my mind at critical times when the grief and despair seemed overwhelming.

Although I'm not the mother of a child who has died, in some small measure, I could understand the agony Whitney was describing that day. As we talked, I shared with her a poem that had brought great insight into what happened to our family when we lost Matthew. Interestingly, the Lord would use this poem I heard on the radio two years after Matthew's death to help me see the truth. The poem, titled "Death Barged In," was written by a woman named Kathleen Sheeder Bonanno after the murder of her daughter.

DEATH BARGED IN

In his Russian greatcoat, slamming open the door with an unpardonable
bang, and he has been here ever since.

He changes everything, rearranges the furniture, his hand hovers by
the phone; he will answer now, he says; he will be the answer.

Tonight he sits down to dinner at the head of the table as we eat, mute;
later, he climbs into bed between us.

Even as I sit here, he stands behind me clamping two colossal hands on
my shoulders and bends down and whispers to my neck:

From now on, You write about me. [41]

As I heard the poem, the thought that came to mind was John 11:25: Jesus is the resurrection and the LIFE! He showed me that we had allowed death to barge in and stay far too long. It was a choice. Matthew was and is eternally alive and well. I had a choice. I could choose life or death. From that day on, I made a conscious choice for LIFE!

As I relayed this story and poem to Whitney, I sensed that when Whitney went to bed for several days at a time, she was listening to the wrong voice and she didn't even know it. I asked Whitney to examine the voice in her head and the thoughts that led to these times of extreme despondency and debilitating depression. I asked her to consider that the thoughts in her head were from the voice of the enemy. The bed symbolized a grave, and the enemy's voice was beckoning her to lie down with him for a few days. She was horrified at the thought. But as she examined the thoughts in her head, she realized they were all connected with depression and death. She realized she had allowed death to barge in and stay. As she prayed and asked the Lord for help, she confessed that the thoughts she had thought were her own and were not the Lord's thoughts. She knew they did not originate with her because she hated the thoughts. She left our time together that day with a resolve that the next time the enemy invited her back to the grave for a few days, she would not go with him.

Several months later, Whitney walked up to me with a big smile on her face and said, "I didn't go. This time, I didn't go. I wanted to. I struggled at first because I felt the depression coming over me, but then I remembered whose voice it was that I was hearing and I didn't go to bed!"

It has been several years now, and to date, Whitney has continued to choose the right voice. Whitney is choosing LIFE!

I have learned that many women do not recognize the source of the voice in their heads. They do not realize the serpent is still speaking (Gen. 3:1). However, once they consider he is still speaking today, the women I am counseling are refusing to cater to his voice. They are beginning to examine the thoughts in their minds and choose God's voice over the voice of the enemy. Note: The enemy's voice can also be identified with the believer's other two enemies, namely: the world and the flesh (Eph. 2:2-3).

WHAT ABOUT YOU?

Do you ever engage in conversation with the enemy?

Be careful how you answer. You may be surprised. It may not be as monumental as the loss of a loved one. But it can be in something as simple as an argument. Let me explain.

A while back, my husband and I were in a heated discussion about something that had occurred. Let me be perfectly honest: I was angry with the way he had behaved. Sadly, for almost two days I rehearsed in my mind over and over again what had been said, done, and not done! Every time I would think I was getting over it, the thoughts would resurface. Unbeknownst to me, I was engaged in a conversation with the enemy, and he was having a heyday and I was in the pit of self-pity.

The more I thought about it, the angrier I became. You see, what I thought affected the way I behaved. I had given him the silent treatment all day. As I write this, I realize just how deceived I really was that day, because this probably was a blessing for my husband. Not only did the things I was thinking about all day affect the way I behaved, but they also affected how I felt. I was miserable!

As we lay in bed that night, I wrestled with another voice in my head. Except this voice brought to mind these words: "Do not let the sun go down on your anger, and do not give the devil an opportunity" (Eph. 4:26–27). I knew the Holy Spirit had brought these verses to mind. You may be asking, "How do you know it was the Holy Spirit speaking to you?" Well, I can assure you I was NOT thinking about the Lord or His Word at this time, and I knew the enemy for sure was not bringing this thought to my mind. So I reluctantly told my husband what the Lord had brought to my mind. Let's just say, things did not get resolved, and we both chose our hurt and anger.

Thankfully, I could not sleep. I looked at the clock, and it was 1:00 a.m. To make matters worse, my husband was sound asleep! I got up in my frustration and went to the den. I cried out to the Lord and asked Him for help. The thought that immediately came to my mind was this: "You have been listening all day to the WRONG voice!" Immediately, I knew that was true. In my deception, I had been engaged in a conversation with the enemy for the past several hours, and the more we conversed, the angrier I had become. The saddest part of all is that I had no idea it was the voice of the enemy. An overwhelming peace ensued as I confessed this to the Lord and asked for His forgiveness. Interestingly, my anger subsided immediately and I was able to go back to bed and sleep in peace.

The next morning, before I could apologize, my husband confessed to me that in his quiet time the Lord brought to his mind that he had been listening to the wrong voice. He apologized for his behavior and asked for my forgiveness. Thankfully, we both confessed our sin, not only to the Lord but also to each other. Amazingly, when the Lord speaks through His Word, there is truth—and truth sets free! We were both set free from anger and the lies and deception of the enemy, and peace returned to our home.

Now let's go back to Genesis 3.

    b. What exactly does Eve say to the serpent in verses 2–3?

1) From the fruit of the trees of the garden _____

BUT . . .

2) From the fruit of the tree which is in the _____ of the garden,

GOD HAS SAID, _____

OR

_____

lest you _____ .

c. Now, compare what she said with what God said. Is this what God said? Explain.

_____

_____

_____

You might be saying to yourself, "Well, she got pretty close to what God said. She only added one thing." Let's consider the one thing she added, only three little words: "or touch it." Have you ever pondered the significance of the words she added? Think about it. What has to happen before you eat something? You have to touch it first!

Now let's consider the verses directly AFTER she touched the fruit. Genesis 3:6 states, "When the woman saw that the tree was good for food, and that it was a delight to the eyes, and that the tree was desirable to make one wise, **she took from its fruit and ate**" (emphasis added). If Eve believes that touching the fruit meant death, and she touches it and nothing happens, she is left to doubt God's word and is open to listen to the voice of the enemy. Could the serpent be correct? The logical conclusion makes her think that if she touched it and nothing happened, maybe—just maybe—she can eat it and nothing will happen as well.

PROBLEM #2—SHE DID NOT KNOW THE WORD OF GOD.

Clearly, one cannot overestimate the necessity of truly knowing God's Word! Let us consider the words of Moses as he instructed the children of Israel just before his death: "Take to your heart all the words with which I am warning you today, which you shall command your sons to observe carefully, even all the words of this law. For it is not an idle word for you; indeed it is your life" (Deut. 32:46-47). God's Word is not an idle word; it is our life!

Now let's consider the importance of the location of the tree. Why do you think He placed it in the MIDDLE of the garden? I believe God placed it in the middle of the garden so that it would be a visible reminder. He didn't hide it in a remote corner of the garden, as the enemy might have done. Everything the enemy does is hidden. Everything the Lord does is in the open!

Furthermore, another tree named in the middle of the garden was the tree of life (Gen. 2:9). We were never forbidden to eat from that tree. Had we only obeyed God's word and eaten freely from every tree but the one forbidden, man would have eventually eaten from the tree of life and lived. Thankfully, although man's downfall began with a tree, his ascent ends with a tree—the cross.

EXAMINING THE HEART FROM GENESIS 3

Part Two: The Will

Have you ever considered what might have happened if Adam and Eve had exercised faith in God's word? If they would have chosen to listen to God's voice and surrender their wills to His will and walk in obedience to His command? They would have continued to have fellowship with the God who created them. The inward surrender of their wills would have resulted in an outward obedience. In essence, they would have fulfilled the purpose for which He had created them. That purpose is to bring Him glory (Isa. 43:7). But we all know that did not happen.

Let's examine what did happen by looking intently at Genesis 3, specifically in regard to the will of man.

GENESIS 3:6–13

1. Look at Genesis 3:6 and record what Eve did.

   a. _____

   and

   b. _____

   What do you see in her act of sin immediately? _____

2. Looking at Genesis 3:6, what did Adam do? _____

3. Let's examine the consequences of their sinful choice. Look at Genesis 3:7 and record what happened specifically to their eyes.

The Hebrew word for *evil* is *ra'*, which comes from a root meaning "to spoil," "to break in pieces"—being broken, and so, made worthless. It's meaning is much broader than sin.[42]

In the Greek, the words *kakos* and *ponēros* are used for evil. *Kakos* is defined as "one who is evil in himself and, as such, gets others in trouble."[43] In the New Testament, *kakos* and *ponēros* mean, respectively, the quality of evil in its essential character and its hurtful effects or influence.[44]

4. What do you think their eyes were opened to when you consider the meaning of the word *evil* in both the Hebrew and Greek languages?

_____

_____

Now let's look at their response to evil.

5. Adam and Eve responded specifically in three distinct ways after they had disobeyed the Lord.

   a. What was their first response according to Genesis 3:7?

_____

_____

   b. What was their second response according to Genesis 3:8?

_____

_____

   c. Now, as we look at the third response, we will need to consider Adam and Eve separately.

      1) What did Adam say in Genesis 3:12? _____

_____

      2) What specifically is Adam doing in this verse? _____

      3) Who specifically is he blaming?

     _____

    and

     _____

      4) What does Eve say when questioned by the Lord God in Genesis 3:13? ____

   a. What specifically is Eve doing in this verse? _____

   b. Who specifically is she blaming? _____

Do you see the three responses to sin?

Isn't that what we do?

Truly, every time sin is the choice, man will choose to

Cover
Hide
Blame

If you are not certain whether sin is involved, trace it backward by asking the Lord, "Am I covering, hiding, or blaming someone or something else?" If the answer is yes to the question, you can be sure sin is the root issue!

Scripture declares, "As [a man] thinks within himself, so he is" (Prov. 23:7).

Eve's choice to listen to the voice of the enemy clearly affected her decision to disobey the voice of the Lord. In essence, she chose the voice of the enemy over the Lord's voice. Similarly, Adam chose to listen to the voice of his wife, fully knowing it was in direct opposition to what the Lord had said to him.

As a result of their sinful choice, Scripture states, "Then the eyes of both of them were opened, and they knew that they were naked" (Gen. 3:7). Now, for the first time, Adam and Eve's eyes were opened and they had an experiential knowledge of evil. What they did next is indicative of what we do when we have sinned.

The first choice they made was an attempt to *cover* their sin. Genesis 3:7 states, "And they sewed fig leaves together and **made themselves loin coverings**" (emphasis added). Secondly, "when they heard the sound of the LORD God walking in the garden . . . the man and his wife **hid themselves** from the presence of the LORD God among the trees of the garden" (Gen. 3:8, emphasis added). Thirdly, when questioned by the LORD God, they each proceeded to blame. Adam blamed both the LORD God and Eve: "The woman whom **Thou** gavest to be with me, **she gave me** from the tree, and I ate" (Gen. 3:12, emphasis added). Likewise, Eve began to place blame: "The **serpent** deceived me, and I ate" (Gen. 3:13, emphasis added).

Lest we become critical, we must realize that we respond to sin in the same way. We cover, hide, and blame others. This is the universal response to sin, and it is as old as the garden.

WHAT ABOUT YOU?

As you have worked through this lesson, has the Holy Spirit pinpointed anything in your life you are covering, hiding, or blaming on someone or something else?

What is it? _____

_____

_____

_____

If the Holy Spirit has brought something to your mind, write it down. Many times, people who are being counseled will read these passages, become convicted of sin in their lives, and then say something like, "I've NEVER told anyone this before, but . . ."

If that's you, keep reading!

EXAMINING THE HEART FROM GENESIS 3

Part Three: Emotions

To complete the study on Genesis 3 and the heart, we will need to consider the emotional aspect of the heart. Oftentimes, when it comes to emotions, women, in general, tend to get a bad rap. However, because the heart is not gender-specific, men can also be led or controlled by their emotions. The issue is not that we have emotions; rather, the issue lies in the high place we give them. In other words, we can get into all kinds of trouble when we allow ourselves to be led by our emotions.

Because our hearts are comprised of the mind, will, and emotions, we need to recognize that emotions are not bad or evil. In fact, the emotional component of our heart was the Creator's intention and plan **before** the fall of man.

1. Let's look at the emotional state of Adam and Eve **before** the Fall. In Genesis 2:25, Adam and Eve's state of being is described by an adjective ("naked") and a verb ("not ashamed"). List them below.

   a. _____

   b. _____

2. What can these two descriptions tell us about their emotional state? _____

Would it be fair to assume that when one is "naked and . . . not ashamed," there would be feelings of great love, exceeding joy, and perfect peace?

Furthermore, the fellowship they enjoyed with the LORD God had a direct correlation with the fellowship they shared with each other. So what happened? We need not go far to find out. The very next verse in Scripture describes exactly what happened. In fact, the innocence of man is seen in direct contrast with the craftiness of the serpent (Gen. 3:1).

Before man's encounter with the serpent, his mind was being directed by God's voice, which, in turn, was leading his will in obedience, leaving man in the emotional state of peace and joy. In short, the heart of man was functioning in the way God intended.

However, listening to the voice of the enemy will lead man not only to a change of mind and will but also to a drastic change in emotions. When the emotions are in charge of the will and the mind, chaos and confusion ensue. In other words, the heart will be out of order and soon become very sick.

In the last section of the chapter, we examined man's response after he had sinned. His response is the universal response to all sin. Specifically, mankind will do the following:

1) Cover

2) Hide

3) Blame

Now let's consider the emotional state of man in regard to these specific responses to sin.

1. Look at Genesis 3:7. What emotions would be attached to the knowledge that they were naked and the corresponding attempt to cover? _____

2. Look at Genesis 3:8. What emotions would be attached in their attempt to hide from God? _____

3. And last, look at Genesis 3:12–13. What emotions are driving them to blame everyone but themselves? _____

WHAT ABOUT YOU?

Think about it. When you choose to sin . . .

Why do you cover? _____

Why do you hide? _____

Why do you blame others? _____

The emotional response to sin is clearly stated in Scripture. Adam and Eve covered themselves because they were afraid and ashamed (Gen. 3:7). Similarly, they hid themselves because they were afraid and felt the guilt of that shame (Gen. 3:10). And last, fear and anger became the emotional responses for blaming God and others. Fear is the overarching emotional response to sin! When we have a proper fear of God, we will surrender our wills to His Word and obey Him. When we fear God, we do not struggle with the fear of other things.

Moreover, man's universal response to sin targets everyone but himself.

- When we attempt to cover, it is always *from one another.*

- When we hide, it is always *from God.*

- When we blame, *God, others,* and *Satan* become the targets.

Just as man was never meant to experientially know evil, he was also never meant to experience the emotional responses of fear, shame, guilt, and anger. If only man had chosen to obey the voice of the Lord.

The same is true today.

Men and women alike are becoming increasingly paralyzed with fear, shame, guilt, and anger.

To make matters worse, there seems to be little difference among those who profess Christ as their Lord and Savior.

Sadly, the counsel of the church is increasingly choosing a more psychiatric approach for treatment, mixed with a few Bible verses here and there as a solution. By choosing to cope rather than seeking a cure, many of the believers I counsel are medicating their fear, shame, guilt, and anger with little to no relief. In fact, many become worse. When sin is the issue, there is a cure—the cross. Jesus is the Sin-Bearer. He died to take upon Himself our sin so that we do not have to bear it because we can't.

Similarly, behavior modification is also presented as a means to help "control" one's emotions. We are being fed the lie that we must simply change our behavior, when, in fact, the behavior is never the issue. The issue is always the heart!

So where do we go for biblical counsel?

Many in the church are running everywhere but to the Lord of the Word and the Word of the Lord for counsel.

Isaiah, prophesying about the coming Messiah, states, "For a child will be born to us, a son will be given to us; and the government will rest on His shoulders; and His name will be called **Wonderful Counselor** . . ." (Isa. 9:6, emphasis added).

Similarly, as Isaiah describes the Spirit who would rest on Him, he states, "And the Spirit of the LORD will rest on Him, the spirit of wisdom and understanding, **the spirit of counsel** and strength, the spirit of knowledge and the fear of the LORD" (Isa. 11:2, emphasis added).

Likewise, the psalmist declares, "Thy testimonies also are my delight; **they are my counselors**" (Ps. 119:24, emphasis added). As far as I can tell, the Father, the Lord Jesus, His Spirit, and the Word of God are the only true counselors.

The Scriptures declare that true counsel and wisdom come from the One "in whom are hidden all the treasures of wisdom and knowledge" (Col. 2:3). Therefore, biblical counsel is available to those who believe in Him by the power of His Spirit, using the Word of God. So why is the church running elsewhere for counsel? We listen to other voices in our heads because we do not know His voice (His Word). Isn't that what happened in the garden? Eve's reply to the enemy's voice confirms that she did not know what God had said. By entering into a conversation with the enemy, she was led to doubt God's word and His character.

As I have prayerfully contemplated Genesis 3 in regard to the heart, two aspects have clearly emerged and need to be understood: the *foundation* and the *framework* for true biblical counseling are found in Genesis 3. In this chapter we have established the biblical foundation of Genesis 3 in regard to the heart, and in the next chapter we will look at the biblical framework provided within Genesis 3.

Do you see it?

If you were to organize the foundational truths you have discovered in this chapter from Genesis 3 regarding the heart, it would look like the following:

THE BIBLICAL FRAMEWORK OF GENESIS 3 AND THE HEART		
Mind	Will	Emotions
God's Voice "From any tree of the garden you may eat freely" BUT . . . "From the tree of the knowledge of good and evil *You shall not eat *You shall surely die" (Gen. 2:16–17)	**Obedience to God's Word** **Naked**—(Gen. 2:25) **Not ashamed**–(Gen. 2:25)	**Fellowship** Fear of God Love Joy Peace
Satan's Voice "Indeed, has God said, 'You shall not eat from any tree in the garden'?" "You surely shall not die!" "For God knows that in the day you eat from it *Your eyes will be opened *You will be like God, knowing good and evil" (Gen. 3:1, 4–5)	**Disobedience to God's Word** **Cover**—"sewed fig leaves together and made themselves loin coverings" (Gen. 3:7) **Hide**—"hid themselves from the presence of the LORD God" (Gen. 3:8) **Blame**—"The woman whom Thou gavest to be with me, she gave me from the tree, and I ate." (Gen. 3:12) "The serpent deceived me, and I ate." (Gen. 3:13)	**Separation** Fear/Shame Fear/Guilt Fear/Anger

CHAPTER 6

HOW TO OVERCOME THE EVIL ONE

PART TWO: ESTABLISHING THE BIBLICAL FRAMEWORK USING GENESIS 3

"But I am afraid, lest as the serpent deceived Eve by his craftiness, your *minds should be led astray* from the *simplicity* and *purity* of devotion to Christ."

(2 Cor. 11:3, emphasis added)

As the Holy Spirit unveiled the heart of man in Genesis 3, I was overwhelmed! I began to contemplate this incredible picture of the heart. Over the course of the next several hours, the process of how this serves as the framework for spiritual counseling began to unfold in my mind. The following is what the Spirit of truth illuminated.

First, He focused my attention on the emotions of fear, shame, guilt, and anger. The thought that came to my mind was "This is how the women who come for counsel present themselves." How true! Every woman I have ever counseled comes in with a heart that is being led by her emotions. He illuminated the fact that the common denominator with each particular emotion was fear. Immediately, 2 Timothy 1:7 came to mind.

1. Look at 2 Timothy 1:7 and record the verse.

_____

_____

_____

2. Now, answer the following questions using 2 Timothy 1:7.

   a. What is the spirit specifically called in this verse? _____

   b. If God has not given a "spirit of fear" (NKJV), from where is this spirit coming?

   _____

   _____

   c. What are the characteristics God's Spirit has given?
      1) _____

      2) _____

      3) _____

   d. Now think with me. What are the opposite characteristics of God's Spirit using this verse?
      1) Instead of power – _____

      2) Instead of love – _____

      3) Instead of discipline (sound mind) – _____

People who are presenting with their emotions in charge are oftentimes bound with a spirit of fear (or "timidity") that manifests itself characteristically in weakness and even paralysis, hatred, or discord, and many will say, "I feel like I am going crazy." Clearly, their emotions are in charge!

Second, I saw the need to "back the counselee up." In other words, I wanted to use the foundational chart of Genesis 3, located on page 63, as a framework from which to counsel. For example, start with the presenting emotions of fear, shame, guilt, and anger. These are not difficult to discover. Emotions are always the presenting symptoms from which to start because they are so visible. The emotions are the obvious baggage we tend to carry around. Each emotion can be "backed up" to the section on the chart regarding the will. The emotional responses directly correspond to the areas in our lives that we are covering, hiding, or blaming on others. This is man's universal response to sin. Therefore, the emotions are the aftermath of sin.

In other words, the issue is not the emotions. Oftentimes, this is where we want to camp out. If you think about it, the emotions of fear, shame, guilt, and anger are the things we medicate. These are the things we focus on in any given counseling situation. But the presenting problem is never THE problem. The problem is a root, which will be attached to something that the counselee is **covering**, **hiding**, or **blaming** on others.

At this point, I cannot overemphasize enough the need to pray and ask the Holy Spirit to guide you to the truth about what you are covering and hiding, or whom you are blaming. You will not see this on your own.

MY STORY

I will never forget the day the Lord illuminated this truth to me personally. I had just fed all four children and was rushing to get out of the house when my oldest daughter dropped a partial gallon of milk on the floor that I had just mopped. She was about nine years old at the time. I will NEVER forget the look on her sweet face as I began to go into a tirade. With a very loud voice I began to literally rake her over the coals for her carelessness. Her face will forever be imprinted on my mind as I saw for the first time fear in her eyes and deep hurt as she watched me throw my fit. One of the most frightening things of all is that the longer I ranted, the more control I lost. Sometimes, in these fits of anger, I would curse. I remember thinking, *Even if I wanted to stop, I couldn't.* I would tell myself things like *No one is perfect* and *I am only human.* I would rationalize that the outbursts were rare and sporadic since they would surface about two to three times a year. But this day was different. This time I had exploded in front of my child. This time my anger was directed at one of the most precious gifts God had given me. Needless to say, I was distraught!

As I looked at the fear I had invoked in her, I left the room and went straight to my bedroom. I locked the door and fell on my face before the Lord and cried out to the Lord for help. I remember telling Him that if He didn't rescue me from this anger, my children would not only suffer but be deeply scarred and ruined for life. I was desperate for help!

As I look back at that time in my life, I realize the Lord was wanting to uproot and destroy the things in my life that were not from Him so that He could built and plant (Jer. 1:10). I needed a SAVIOR—not concerning my eternal destiny but for that moment in time. In other words, I did not need to be saved from the penalty of sin. I had already been justified the day I heard the gospel and received Christ as my Savior and Lord. What I needed that day was to be saved from the power I had allowed sin to take in my life. This is the process of sanctification. At that time, I could not have explained what was happening to me, but I realize now that the Holy Spirit was crying out for me on my behalf. He is the reason I was able to pray and ask the Lord for His perspective on my angry outbursts. Instead of reacting to others and blaming them for "making me angry," I realized that the issue was within me. Only the Holy Spirit can reveal this truth.

No one could have prepared me for what He showed me. In all honesty, He had brought this to my mind before, but I dismissed the idea because I thought one thing had nothing to do with the other. This time, it was different. I knew without a doubt that this was the source of my anger.

Immediately after I cried out to the Lord, He brought to my mind a memory that I had tried to erase for years—a memory that no one knew. Shame and guilt began to flood my mind. I began to feel overwhelmed with a paralyzing fear. I remember thinking immediately afterward that once this horrible memory was out, I could not take it back.

We had moved to Fort Smith, Arkansas, when I was in junior high school. I found myself in a new environment that was very different from the one I had left. I was extremely naive, even to the point of sheer ignorance. I used to console myself with the thought that because I was ignorant and didn't know any better, I was somehow vindicated from my sin. Unfortunately, it did not change the way I felt, nor did it excuse what I had done.

I was frightened to attend another school. However, that all changed as I began to make new friends and get settled into a new place. I soon became excited and caught off guard when I realized I had gained the attention of a guy a year older than me. Before I knew it, we were "going out." After a time, he began to tell me things like, "If you really love me, you will . . ." I remember having thoughts like *If I don't do what he wants, he will break up with me*. These thoughts began to control my mind, and to the mind of a fifteen year old, this seemed unbearable. I remember feeling uncomfortable about it all, but I really did want to show him how much I loved him (or thought I did). Instead of going to my parents for counsel, I turned to my peers, who quickly informed me that it was "no big deal" and "everyone was doing it." I had never been told about the "facts of life." I had never had "the talk" with my parents. I do not say this to blame my parents, but I say this because ignorance is not bliss. An ignorant heart can lead to sin just as easily as a rebellious one.

After several months of persuasion, I relented and gave away the one thing I could never get back. Immediately, I felt dirty and used, especially when right afterward, he broke up and moved on. My heart was devastated! To make matters worse, I could not share this with anyone. Guilt and shame overwhelmed me.

Paul warns about this in 1 Corinthians 6:18: "Flee immorality. Every other sin that a man commits is outside the body, but the immoral man **sins against his own body**" (emphasis added). Alongside the part of the verse with the words "sins against his own body," I have written in the flyleaf of my Bible, "my mind." For the part of my body most affected by this immoral sin has been my mind!

Unfortunately, my sin did not end there. With a broken heart, I convinced myself to try to replace this guy I had loved and trusted so much. So I turned to another whom I had no feelings for whatsoever for relief, and I was immoral with him. Immediately afterward, he dumped me too.

By this time, I had sworn off ALL boys. I said that I would NEVER do that again. I would NEVER trust another guy again. I was overwhelmed with grief and shame all over again. I covered my sin with lies and hid my sin from everyone—except the Lord, of course. Many months later, I met the man I would marry. He was three years older and had graduated high school. He was more mature than any other guy I had known. He was also very cute and was playing college baseball on a scholarship. I had determined ahead of time that this relationship would be different.

Six months after we met, I realized I was beginning to have strong feelings for him. Knowing this was getting serious, I sat him down and explained to him about my relation-ship with the Lord. I told him if we were to continue dating, he would have to go to church with me. Although he hesitated a bit, he agreed to attend a Wednesday evening youth service. Amazingly, and in the providence of a kind and merciful God, he heard the gospel for the first time and was convicted. I could tell something was different. He was very quiet and withdrawn the rest of the evening. He seemed unsettled.

It was not until the next day that I learned just how troubled he really was. I had met him at his house to feed baseballs into a pitching machine that had been set up in his backyard. Typical date—sounds like a lot of fun, huh? He was unusually serious and quiet. After some time, he went in to shower. I was in the den talking to his parents when he came out and asked, "Can we go to see your youth pastor? I need to talk to him." After the shock dissipated, I called my youth pastor, and he and his wife invited us over. I will never forget the salvation of my boyfriend and future husband. It was one of those rare and dramatic moments ingrained in my mind. I witnessed an eighteen-year-old man literally fall to his knees and cry out as he asked Jesus to be the Savior and Lord of his life. It was a holy moment. It was an exhilarating experience to behold. He would never be the same. We would never be the same.

After three years of dating, we were married. He was a virgin. Sadly, he thought he was marrying a virgin. I had lied to him and told him that I was a virgin. I had done a good job covering and hiding my sin, or at least I thought I had. And so there our life began, but it was based on my lie. One thing you must know: truth will NEVER build on a lie!

Fast-forward to the angry outburst I described earlier. By now it is evident what the Holy Spirit had "put His finger" on in my life. This twenty-year-old "secret" was about to be revealed. At first, I did not see the correlation with my sin and my anger. However, I sensed the Holy Spirit was directing me to bring the secret out into the light. I have since learned that the things that are hidden in our hearts are never hidden from the Lord. I knew these truths in my head, but bringing them to the light brought understanding to my heart.

1. Look at Daniel 2:22 and record what you learn about the Lord God. _____

_____

2. Look at Hebrews 4:13 and record what you learn about the Lord God. _____

_____

Prayerfully consider Daniel 2:22 and Hebrews 4:13. Is there anything we can cover or hide from the Lord? Everyone answering this question will say, "Of course not!" However, how many of us are attempting to cover from others or hide from God something right now? Who are you blaming?

I have also learned that the things that are hidden in the darkness are actually in the domain where the enemy dwells. He dwells in darkness. The Lord is the Light. The enemy will not come anywhere near the Light! I sensed the Holy Spirit was leading me to tell my husband. My sin had affected us, and the Lord wanted to heal us. You may ask, "How do you know it was the Holy Spirit?" Believe me, I really thought long and hard about this. Finally it came down to a series of questions I asked myself:

1. Would the enemy want me to confess this sin and ask for forgiveness? The obvious answer is "Of course not!"

2. Do I want to confess this sin that has been hidden for twenty years to my husband? Absolutely NOT!

3. Whose voice is left?

The answer was obvious to me. However, I have to admit, I honestly could not see anything good coming from this. Little did I know, the Lord would turn it for good and use it to help others who were struggling. In a complete surrender of my will and out of obedience to what I sensed the Holy Spirit was leading me to do, I confessed to my husband the truth after twenty years of lying. I can honestly say I did so out of an immense love for the Lord. Jesus' words "If anyone loves Me, he will keep My word" (John 14:23) gripped my heart and would not let go.

My husband was shocked, hurt, and angry. He did not speak to me for days. At first I thought, "Oh no, what have I done?" I had a fear that he might leave me. Thankfully, he stayed. It has taken some time, but the Lord has healed our marriage exceedingly and abundantly above all that I could have ever asked or imagined. It is built on truth, and the truth sets free (John 8:32).

One thing I noticed immediately: the angry outbursts left, and they have not resurfaced since! Even my three younger children have no recollection of my anger. My son said to me one day, "Mom, I know you say you had anger issues, and I believe you, but that is so hard to imagine because I have never seen in you what you are describing." All I can say to that is PRAISE THE DELIVERER of my soul!

I also want to share that it was imperative that I tell my husband because I sensed the Lord leading me to share with my children what NOT to do. I did not want my children to be ignorant of the truth. I did not want them to live with baggage that would weigh them down and affect their marriages. I cringe at the thought that, at times, I am the example of what not to do; nevertheless, it is true.

And so, one by one, at the appropriate time, each of them was told what not to do and why. My daughters were told at the age I had committed the sin. I don't know why, but I had a more difficult time telling my son. I was able to share with him when the Lord opened a door of opportunity as my son confessed some of his own personal struggles one day. I remember imploring each of them to be "filled with the knowl edge of His will in all spiritual wisdom and understanding, so that [they] may walk in a manner worthy of the Lord, to please Him in all respects, bearing fruit in every good work and increasing in the knowledge of God; strengthened with all power, according to His glorious might, for the attaining of all steadfastness and patience; joyously giving thanks to the Father" (Col. 1:9–12). I did this so they would not ignorantly or willfully choose to live with the baggage I had carried for so long.

Similarly, the Lord showed me the need to ask the two guys from my past for forgiveness. I knew I had sinned against the Lord, but I had also sinned against them. We rarely sin in isolation. Two things of importance must be noted here: (1) I did not contact these men without the permission of my husband; and (2) I did not in any way blame them. I simply owned my sin and asked for their forgiveness. This was in no way a means of reconnecting. It was a simple (yet extremely difficult) act of obedience TO THE LORD!

You may be reading and thinking, *This is quite drastic.* I realize many may believe this is unnecessary and even radical. I would agree, or at least that is what I told the Lord until He showed me His perspective from His Word. In Scripture, Jesus is asked by one of the Pharisees, "Which is the great commandment?" (Matt. 22:36). Jesus answers him by saying, "'You shall love the Lord your God with all your heart, and with all your soul, and with all your mind.' This is the great and foremost commandment. The second is like it, 'You shall love your neighbor as yourself'" (Matt. 22:37–39). The Lord used these verses to teach me that my sin had affected my relationship with Him. Because I was His child, my sin had involved Him. It had separated me from the sweet fellowship I had once known in my innocence. I had spent years asking for His forgiveness (although I knew He forgave me the moment I asked). However, my sin had also involved others. I had never asked for their forgiveness. He showed me that by not asking for their forgiveness it was still affecting my relationship with Him, for the two were inseparable. This new (to me) insight from His Word caused great distress. I knew that to exercise faith in God's Word, I would have to surrender my will to His will and walk in obedience to His Word. I cannot even begin to tell you the great struggle that occurred between my will and His will. I remember finally coming to the conclusion that He will never ask me to do more than He did. My mind immediately went to the Garden of Gethsemane, where Jesus lived the ultimate struggle of wills and won the battle. He reminded me that He was in me to empower and enable me to accomplish His will. I cannot even begin to describe to you how I felt when I sensed His pleasure the moment I obeyed Him completely.

3. Look at Hebrews 11:6 and record the verse.

_____

_____

_____

_____

HE is the reward for those who by faith seek Him! Many who hear this may say, "Well, that's going a bit too far." But I have to respond by saying, "How far is too far?"

Richard Owen Roberts, in his book *Repentance*, concurs. He wrote:

> Every repentant sinner must go back through his life of sin and ascertain whether or not there are cases in his past where he can still go and repair the damage done. Wherever it is possible to make restitution, to make wrong right, the truly repentant will do so. If someone thinks he has repented and yet he will not make restitution, that person is deceiving himself.[45]

What would the church look like if, when we sinned against others, we actually went to the ones involved and asked for their forgiveness? So often we will run privately to the Lord, but we refuse to go to those we have sinned with or against. I wonder what would happen in the church if we would exercise these two commands of the Lord?

Likewise, how would you feel if the one who had sinned against you or with you asked for your forgiveness? Would healing not occur as a result? And the beautiful thing is this: whether the person you ask for forgiveness accepts or rejects you is not your concern. The offense is between you and the Lord. If they accept your sincere request for forgiveness, will reconciliation not occur? If they choose not to accept, this matter is between them and the Lord. Only He can deal with the heart. You can walk away, knowing that you loved Him enough to obey Him (John 14:23).

In retrospect, the anger I had been plagued with for so long was really anger I had had toward myself. Outwardly, it manifested in me in perfectionism. Inwardly, it revealed a hidden shame and guilt that manifested itself in anger toward anything in my life that was not perfect. It made me critical of others and very judgmental. Unknowingly, we criticize others for the very things we inwardly hate about ourselves. We think that putting the spotlight on others and their sins will take the focus off us. And we do all this, never realizing we are the ones deceived. When I allowed the Lord to heal my inward heart, I could let go of the outward need for perfection. He filled my heart with compassion and love for others.

I guess you could say, the day I went into a rage, literally over spilled milk, was the day I dehisced! The term *dehisce* is a medical term that means the spontaneous opening of a wound that has not healed because of infection. Praise the Lord, the Great Physician was there. Praise the Lord, He took the scalpel of His Word and lanced my pus-filled heart so that I could heal. And now, I am left with a scar. Thankfully, scars don't hurt. They are merely reminders of a time of great hurt and merciful healing!

A WORD OF CAUTION

At this point, I sense a word of caution would be not only helpful but necessary. First and foremost, all sin is against the Lord. Therefore, He must deal with it first. However, if another person (or more than one person) is involved in your sin, you must go to them and seek forgiveness. As a general rule, "a sin should be confessed as widely as the influence of that sin has spread."[46] In other words, if you are contacting someone who has no idea of the offense, leave the offense between you and the Lord. Going to another person who has no idea about your sin will only cause hurt and confusion. You should only contact those who are involved and have been hurt and affected by your sin.

Roberts, citing the *Westminster Confession of Faith*, states,

> As every man is bound to make private confession of his sins to God, praying for the pardon thereof; upon which, and the forsaking of them, he shall find mercy; so he that scandalizeth his brother, or the Church of

Christ, ought to be willing, by a private or public confession, and sorrow for his sin, to declare his repentance to those that are offended, who are thereupon to be reconciled to him, and in love to receive him.[47]

Another word of caution is needful. When you have sinned against another person, do not go to them and say, "*If* I have offended you, I am sorry." There is no *if* about an offense. You have either offended someone or you have not. Using the word *if* only causes more hurt, and it shifts the blame from you to them. Own your sin. Take responsibility for what you have done and make it right before the Lord and the one(s) offended.

There have been times when I know a person is clearly offended, but I am unaware of what I did or said. At this point, I ask them to tell me. I take full responsibility and am quick to ask for their forgiveness because I know I am capable of saying and doing things, even if unintentional, that can hurt others. Here's a good precept to consider: "If possible, so far as it depends on you, be at peace with all men" (Rom. 12:18).

And **last**, within the biblical framework provided using Genesis 3, it is imperative to "back up" one step further, to identify the voice to which you have been listening. In other words, after the Holy Spirit has identified the area(s) you have covered, hidden, and/or blamed others for, and you have biblically dealt with each, back up in the chart to the section that considers the voice you listened to before you sinned. This has been the **most transforming truth** the Lord has illumined to me in this process. It is imperative to identify the voice (thoughts) in your head.

And by all means, please know that I am not inciting you toward a "witch hunt." I am in no way suggesting you go back to every sin you have ever committed and try to make amends. What I have personally shared is for those whose past sin is affecting them presently. In other words, you cannot seem to move past it. When this occurs, at least consider that it may be God's Spirit wanting to set your heart free now.

VOICES

For the purpose of understanding the workbook, all references made to hearing God's voice pertain to when the Spirit of God brings a specific passage from Scripture to one's mind that is applicable to the situation. Jesus states, "But the Helper, the Holy Spirit, whom the Father will send in My name, He will teach you all things, and **bring to your remembrance** all that I said to you" (John 14:26, emphasis added). For example, when one is experiencing a time of anxiety and fear, hearing God's voice might involve the Holy Spirit bringing to mind this verse: "The steadfast of mind Thou wilt keep in perfect peace" (Isa. 26:3).

When we ask the Lord to bring to our minds certain truths from our pasts, such as the entry point of a particular emotion, He is well able to bring to our minds a memory or a word that is connected. For example, I was meeting with a woman named Beth who was dealing with the emotion of anger. The anger was clearly connected to her mother. I noticed every time she mentioned her mother, her tone would change. She would blame her mother regardless of the issue being discussed.

When she asked the Lord to lead her to the truth of her anger, He brought to her mind a memory from the past. He reminded her of a time in her early adulthood, after an intense study in the book of John, how the Holy Spirit had impressed on her the need to go to her mother and seek forgiveness for the bitterness and anger she had held in her heart toward her. Her mission from the Lord was to reconcile. She went on to explain that the day she left to obey the Lord, her car broke down. She said, "After my car broke down, I felt impressed that all the Lord really wanted was my obedience to *try* to go. He told me that my mother wouldn't have received it anyway because of the way she was, so I didn't have to go after all." She was sure this was the Lord's voice.

After hearing her describe the memory and her "encounter with the Lord," I perceived several red flags. I had no problem with the first half of the story because it aligns with the truth of God's Word. In the Sermon on the Mount, Jesus stated, "If therefore you are presenting your offering at the altar, and there remember that your brother has something against you, leave your offering there before the altar, and go your way; first be reconciled to your brother, and then come and present your offering" (Matt. 5:23–24). Paul, in his letter to the church at Corinth, urges reconciliation with the Lord, adding, "And He has committed to us the word of reconciliation" (2 Cor. 5:19). Surely being reconciled to the Lord would include reconciliation with others.

However, the second part of her story did not align with God's Word (voice). I reminded her that her mother's response was not the issue. Whether her mother chose to accept or reject her attempt at reconciliation was not her concern. I reminded her that the Lord would have dealt with her mother. Her only job was to obey what the Lord had told her to do, and she was to leave the results to the Lord. I asked her if the car breaking down could have been an attempt by the enemy to keep her from obeying God's voice. She said without hesitation, "Yes." I then asked her to pray and ask the Lord if it was His voice that said, "All I really wanted was your obedience to try to go. Your mother would not have received it anyway." Immediately after praying, she said, "No." She told me these words had come to mind: "You were afraid of being rejected again." She began to weep and said, "My mother is dead now, and it's too late." Thankfully, the story did not end with her in tears with a heart filled with anger and bitterness. It is never too late for forgiveness, as long as you still have breath. Oftentimes, we attribute thoughts in our minds that do not line up with the Word of God. The Word is where He speaks. If a thought in your mind does not align with the truth of God's Word, I can assure you, it is NOT from Him!

Similarly, all references made to hearing the voice of the enemy would include thoughts that are contrary to the Word of God, resulting in doubt, which can eventually lead to acts of disobedience. Jesus warns, "For out of the heart come evil **thoughts**, murders, adulteries, fornications, thefts, false witness, slanders" (Matt. 15:19, emphasis added). Likewise, Paul lists the shield of faith as part of the armor of God, which is "able to extinguish all the **flaming missiles of the evil one**" (Eph. 6:16, emphasis added). The enemy's voice is clearly seen in 2 Corinthians 10:4–5: "For the weapons of our warfare are not of the flesh, but divinely powerful for the destruction of fortresses. We are destroying

speculations and every lofty thing raised up against the knowledge of God, and we are taking every **thought** captive to the obedience of Christ" (emphasis added).

The Puritan writer Thomas Watson, addressing the way the enemy works, stated, "Satan, although he cannot read our minds . . . he can instill evil thoughts into the mind. As the Holy Ghost casts in good suggestions, so the devil casts in bad ones. He put it into Judas' heart to betray Christ (John 13:2)."[48]

For clarification purposes: We started with the presenting emotion(s), which led us to allow the Holy Spirit to identify what we have covered, hidden, or blamed others for, in regard to that specific emotion. And now we need to allow the Holy Spirit to back up what has been covered or hidden or blamed on others to the voice to which we have been listening. Identifying the voice in our heads is crucial to the well-being of our hearts! *Is it well with your soul?*

THE PROCESS USING THE GENESIS 3 CHART

It is important throughout this process to have the chart located on the next page in front of you as you follow the method. You will reference it many times, and it will serve as an excellent visual as you go through the process of learning how to overcome the enemy.

Looking at the chart, **begin with the presenting emotions(s)**, and allow the Holy Spirit to guide you as you "back up" to the left of the chart under the "Will" category. For example, if you are dealing with the emotion of anger, ask the Holy Spirit to pinpoint any area in your life that you may be covering, hiding, or blaming others for. After the Lord has brought to your mind the sin that is connected with the anger, you will need to consult the Word of God to deal with that sin biblically.

For example, as you pray, the Lord may bring to your mind a person or a memory with which you are angry. Oftentimes, the anger is attached to another person(s) who has caused you hurt.

At this point, I would counsel you to pray and ask the Holy Spirit to bring to the surface all the thoughts attached to this hurtful memory or person. This process can take time. Allow the Holy Spirit to get to the root thoughts and issues. Once you have allowed the thoughts to surface and you can visibly see them on paper, you will see where you have held unforgiveness, bitterness, and any other sin that may be hindering your walk with the Lord.

Once you have identified your sin, which will be visible in the way you have responded to this situation/person, you will want to consult God's Word to deal with the sin biblically. After you have surrendered your will and obeyed God's Word in regard to your sin, you will sense immediate relief. You should see the anger leave immediately.

The last step is to back up to the left of the chart under the heading "Mind." You will want to look at the thoughts on your paper and clearly be able to identify the voice behind the sin. This last step is important for future temptation. You will be able to identify the voice of deception by placing it up against the truth of God's Word. I have learned that this is a vital part of the process.

You will be able to readily see that the thoughts that have dominated your mind for so long have affected the way you have responded (your will) and the way you have felt (your emotions).

THE BIBLICAL FRAMEWORK OF GENESIS 3 AND THE HEART		
Mind	Will	Emotions
God's Voice "From any tree of the garden you may eat freely" BUT . . . "From the tree of the knowledge of good and evil *You shall not eat *You shall surely die" (Gen. 2:16–17)	Obedience to God's Word Naked—(Gen. 2:25) Not ashamed–(Gen. 2:25)	Fellowship Fear of God Love Joy Peace
Satan's Voice "Indeed, has God said, 'You shall not eat from any tree in the garden'?" "You surely shall not die!" "God knows that in the day you eat from it *Your eyes will be opened *You will be like God, knowing good and evil" (Gen. 3:1, 4–5)	Disobedience to God's Word Cover—"sewed fig leaves together and made themselves loin coverings" (Gen. 3:7) Hide—"hid themselves from the presence of the LORD GOD" (Gen. 3:8) Blame—"The woman whom Thou gavest to be with me, she gave me from the tree and I ate." (Gen. 3:12) "The serpent deceived me, and I ate." (Gen. 3:13)	Separation Fear/Shame Fear/Guilt Fear/Anger

CHAPTER 7

HOW TO OVERCOME THE EVIL ONE

PART THREE: THE PRACTICAL APPLICATION OF GENESIS 3

"Behold, I have put My words in your mouth. See, I have appointed
you this day over the nations and over the kingdoms, to pluck up and
to break down, to destroy and to overthrow, to build and to plant."

(Jer. 1:9b–10)

These words, which were spoken to Jeremiah when God was calling him to prophesy His word to the nation of Judah, are as applicable and timely today as they were then. I have found in the discipleship process that little to no instruction is given in regard to things in our past that are influencing and even directing the present. We are quick to want to build and plant, but few people are willing to allow the Spirit of God to take the Word of God to pluck up and break down, to destroy and overthrow. In other words, we want the Lord to build on our junk! When we have not biblically dealt with things in our past, we find out quickly that there can be no growth. This is what I find happening in the lives of countless women looking for spiritual discipleship and counsel. They are so bogged down and paralyzed with fear from their past that they cannot move forward. Many women express real doubts about their salvation. Many are medicating their emotions in an effort to merely cope.

If you look closely at Jeremiah 1:10, you will see a distinct order. First, we must realize the power and authority of God's Word. Scripture declares, "So shall My Word be which goes forth from My mouth; it shall not return to Me empty, without accomplishing what I desire, and without succeeding in the matter for which I sent it" (Isa. 55:11). No one else has the power to speak and create from nothing!

Second, we must be willing to allow the Lord to use His Word "to pluck up and to break down" those things in our lives that are impeding our spiritual growth. You may find it interesting that the Hebrew word for "pluck up" literally means to "uproot." In other words, there are things in our hearts that only the Word of God has the power to expose and uproot. The emotions of fear, shame, guilt, and anger are responses to sin in our lives that we cover, hide, or blame on others. These sins, or roots, are a hindrance to our spiritual growth; therefore, they must be exposed.

Consider the following visual.

The branches represent the emotions we can see such as shame, guilt, anger, and fear. The root represents the sin in our lives that we cover, hide, and blame on others. Oftentimes, we focus our attention on the branch instead of getting to the root.

Third, once we have allowed the Spirit of truth to expose the root, He will guide us to the truth from God's Word on how to deal with it. As we surrender our will to God's will

(Word) and choose to walk in obedience to the truth, the sin, or root, will be destroyed and overthrown. One thing I try to remind the women I counsel is the fact that we cannot choose our tragedies, but we can choose our responses. Whether the tragedy is in the past or I am in the middle of it, I want to respond with a surrendered and obedient heart.

And last, as we cooperate with the Spirit of God by surrendering our wills and obeying His Word, He will use that same Word in our lives to build and plant. Everyone who is a true believer has this as our goal. We all want the Lord to build and plant in our lives; however, few are willing to allow Him to use that same Word to pluck up and destroy those things in our lives that do not align with His Word.

If the goal of every true disciple of Christ is to grow in holiness, then we must be willing to allow the Great Physician to use the scalpel of His Word to uproot and destroy those things in our lives that hinder the building and planting of spiritual fruit. In his book *Created to Praise*, pastor and author Derek Prime states, "The way to holiness is basically simple for the Christian indwelt as he is by the Holy Spirit. It is the daily obedience to the will of God as he is guided by the Scriptures and the Holy Spirit's application to his conscience of what he knows to be God's will."[49]

As I consider the words from Jeremiah 1:9b–10, I am reminded of the woman I took care of in the CICU who had been rushed down to the floor just ten days after her open-heart surgery. She barely hung on to life. Sadly, it was the day she was supposed to have gone home. Instead, she had begun to run a fever a few days before and was feeling very sick. Her vital signs that morning were rapidly changing, and things were quickly going downhill. We got the call that her chest had opened up as pus and blood were pouring from her wound. In medical terms, the woman's chest had dehisced. Literally her heart and entire chest cavity was exposed! Rushing her to surgery to close the wound was not an option because of the massive infection that had spread throughout her chest. The only option was to keep her chest open and begin an aggressive attempt to keep her alive. Interestingly, this had all started with one infected cell that spread like gangrene deep inside her chest cavity.

The physician ordered that her rib cage be left open, and sterile washings of her chest cavity were performed several times a day. Every possible antibiotic was ordered and administered around the clock. Anyone entering the room followed the sterile procedure protocol, which included sterile gowns, gloves, and masks to be worn at all times.

No one that day on her medical team thought this woman would survive. Thankfully and miraculously, weeks later, she was taken back to surgery to close her chest cavity. And to the delighted surprise of all the medical staff, three months later, she walked out of the hospital. What had been an infected and pus-filled open wound had turned into a scar that had healed.

I tell you the story of the lady who physically dehisced and almost died that day because this is what oftentimes happens when I meet women who have "spiritually dehisced." These are the women who seek counsel because everything they were able to hold together for a time has now been opened up, and they feel as if they cannot go any further. The fear, guilt, shame, and anger are now in control of their lives and affecting everything and everyone around them, and they have no idea how to stop the "spiritual bleeding." What they were once able to cope with and control has now taken control.

Sometimes, spiritual surgery is necessary for spiritual health. Over time, we can allow things in our hearts that have not been dealt with biblically to fester and infect our entire bodies, making us spiritually sick.

Thankfully, there is a Physician who specializes in the heart! And He uses His scalpel, the Word of God, that is "living and active and sharper than any two-edged sword," that is able to pierce through things that seem to be inseparable such as "soul and spirit . . . joints and marrow," to the very thing man cannot get to or understand, "the thoughts and intentions of the heart" (Heb. 4:12). He can do this because, as the next verse declares, "all are naked and laid bare to the eyes of Him with whom we have to do" (Heb. 4:13). In other words, He knows where the pus pockets in our spiritual hearts are located, and He wants to lance them with the power of His Word so that we can heal. Sure, we will be left with a scar, but scars don't hurt. Pus pockets do!

A NOTE FOR THE COUNSELOR

Practical Application of the Biblical Framework in Genesis 3

It is at this juncture that I want to proceed with caution concerning the process of discipleship counseling, for fear this will become a three- or five-step program. However, for clarity's sake, I will list the process in steps. It is vastly important that you not view this as a formula or a program. It involves the "simplicity and purity of devotion" (2 Cor. 11:3) to a person, the Lord Jesus Christ, through His Spirit and His Word. Truth is a person, and the truth sets us free!

I would also like to address the one counseling in this section as well. Below are suggestions I have learned that may prove helpful to you as you disciple others. Now let's consider the discipleship process as it is outlined in Genesis 3.

Step One: Pray

The first and most important aspect is to begin the counseling time with prayer, asking the Lord, the Counselor, to guide you by the Spirit of truth and lead you to the truth

(John 16:13). This may seem like an obvious way to begin, but you might be surprised to know how infrequently times of counsel begin with prayer.

Step Two: The Word

Next, you will want to go to the Word, specifically, Genesis 3. As you counsel another person, it is vitally important to allow the counselee to see the truths from Scripture for themselves. I usually have them take a blank piece of paper and divide it into three columns. They will methodically search the Scriptures for themselves to fill in the chart. In the end, with your guidance and questions concerning the text, their chart will look like the chart on pages 63 or 76 when it is complete. I have found that handing them a completed chart is not as effective. Their eyes need to be on the pages of God's Word and their minds engaged in what He is saying. It is one thing for me to tell them; it is quite another when the Lord shows them.

In a recent counseling time, I was sitting across from a woman who was in her early fifties. She had been dealing with depression and anxiety for years. She had been to "Christian counseling" for years. She said, "I have been to at least twelve different counselors over the years." When I asked her how many of them had taken her to the Word of God, she stated, "None of them." I was shocked! Not even one "Christian counselor" had taken her to the Word. My next thought and statement to this woman was "How do you receive counsel apart from the Spirit of truth and the Word?" Hence, the reason she was still seeking counsel for truth.

Step Three: Pray Specifically to Identify and Isolate the Emotion

Now, you will need to ask the person you are counseling to prayerfully ask the Lord which emotion(s) He would like to address. For example, the Lord may first bring to your mind the emotion of fear or shame. I have found it is best to take each emotion one by one. Typically, the emotion is linked to a specific sin that the counselee has not dealt with biblically. (At first, it may seem awkward for the counselee to pray out loud. This is important so that the counselor can hear what is being said to the Lord. I have found oftentimes that the women I am counseling are so confused and overwhelmed by their emotions that they forget what to ask. They may not be accustomed to going to Him for counsel. Many of the women I have counseled verbalize doubt that He will even answer them. As they pray aloud, I pray silently. It is usually not long before the emotion is identified and we can proceed.)

Sometimes, the emotion is revealed while you are examining Genesis 3. Sometimes, it is revealed after prayer. Remember, this emotion is the reason they are seeking counsel. However, the emotion is only the presenting issue. The emotion has become the driving force and is directing what they do (their will) and what they think (their mind). The emotion is in charge and is therefore not difficult to identify. Also remember that the presenting issue is never the issue. It will merely help point to what they have covered, hidden, or blamed on others.

Step Four: Pray Specifically to Identify the Connecting Sin That Is Covered, Hidden, and/or Blamed on Others

Once the Lord has pinpointed the emotion(s), they need to be instructed to prayerfully ask the Lord what they have covered from others, hidden from the God, or blamed on everyone but themselves in regard to this particular emotion. To be thorough, this process is done by taking each of the emotions and looking at them one by one.

I have found that many times the counselee is overwhelmed and does not even know where to start. At this juncture, I recommend a blank legal pad.

I have found that one of the MOST HELPFUL tools in a discipleship appointment is a blank legal pad!

At this part of the process, as they continue to pray, instruct them to write down all the thoughts that come to their mind. For example, when I am counseling someone who is struggling with fear and shame as the presenting emotion, I will instruct the counselee to pray and ask the Lord what she is **covering** in regard to fear. This is best achieved as she writes down her fearful thoughts one by one. I will encourage her to write down the thoughts that come to mind no matter how crazy, embarrassing, or even despicable they may be. She is then instructed to divide her legal pad down the middle. Taking each thought that has come to mind, she is then asked to evaluate each thought with Scripture.

You will want them to continue this process by asking the Lord to reveal ways they have **hidden** their fear and then who they are **blaming** as a result of their fear.

A visual may be helpful here. On the following page you will find an actual list from a woman I was counseling regarding the fear in her life. Notice her first fear. This went on for several pages.

You will need to remind the counselee that each time they ask the Spirit of truth to lead them to the truth, they will need to stop and just listen. I cannot stress the importance of this step enough. Prayer is not one-sided. It is not merely bringing our petitions before Him. He is a person. He has gone to great lengths to restore a sin-severed relationship. Our access to the throne of God was costly! Prayer involves communicating with the Lord and allowing Him to communicate with us. Therefore, they must have their Bible open when they pray. The Word of God is where and how He will speak. Without the Spirit of truth leading through the Word, there is really no place to go. Our complete reliance is on the Counselor. Remember—you are not Him!

I must add a word of caution here. When you pray and ask the Lord to lead you to truth, He will ONLY use His Word to speak. You are not listening for new revelation because there is no new revelation. Hebrews 1:1–2 states clearly, "God, after He spoke long ago to the fathers in the prophets in many portions and in many ways, in these last days has spoken to us in His Son." Jesus Christ, the living Word, is God's final word!

I have found that, at first, this may seem awkward. We are not accustomed to listening for the Lord's voice. Jesus said, "My sheep hear My voice, and I know them, and they follow

THINGS I FEAR

1. Fearful of writing these fears down
2. Fearful of death
3. Fearful of my husband dying
4. Fearful of my children dying
5. Fearful of the unknown
6. Fearful of what God may allow in my life/family's life
7. Fearful of what God calls "good"
8. Fearful of health issues & cancer, chronic sickness, etc.
9. Fearful of something tragic happening to my family (dad, mom, siblings)
10. Fearful of the dark
11. Fearful of being attacked, raped, burglarized, etc.
12. Fearful of tight/closed spaces
13. Fearful of inclement weather: tornado, ice, etc.
14. Fearful of being in a car wreck/someone I know in a wreck
15. Fearful of not being able to raise my children
16. Fearful of being deceived concerning my salvation
17. Fearful of displeasing the Lord
18. Fearful of replaced/forgotten
19. Fearful of children being kidnapped
20. Fearful of where the Lord may send us for international missions
21. Fearful of children not coming to a saving knowledge of the Lord
22. Fearful of the future
23. Fearful of pain, discomfort/suffering
24. Fearful of finding one of my children not breathing/dead in bed
25. Fearful of choking
26. Fearful of one of my children choking and not being able to help
27. Fearful of my husband being tempted/unfaithful/led astray
28. Fearful of losing eyesight/hearing or being paralyzed

Me" (John 10:27). Just a note here: the voice of the Lord is NOT audible. Typically, He will bring a word, thought, or memory to mind. Remember, if the thought in your mind does not align with the Word of God, it is not God speaking!

After a time of listening, I will ask them what the Lord brought to mind. You will be amazed at what He will bring to mind. I have found oftentimes that the counselee barely gets the words out of her mouth before the answer is given. Once the Lord has revealed the sin, it is time to go to the Word for the Lord's perspective and the biblical solution. You will never find the answer to the issue without His perspective.

Examples of Listening to the Lord for Direction

At this point in the process, I think it would be beneficial to give you examples of the process as it is described in step 4. For instance, one day after I taught a Bible study, a woman approached me after class. She was overwhelmed by the thought of death. At one point in our conversation, she said, "Death is all around me. Everyone who is close to me has died. I have thoughts about death all the time, and it is now affecting my child." I asked her to pray and ask the Holy Spirit to lead her to the truth about death—specifically when it entered. In a very hesitant voice she replied, "Now? You want me to pray out loud right now?" I reminded her that I was not the counselor and that only He knew the root of her fear. She prayed and asked the Lord when death had entered. She barely got the words out of her mouth when she looked up at me and said, "I have never told anyone this before, but the Lord brought to mind something I did when I was nineteen years old." With tears in her eyes and her hands visibly trembling, she stated, "He brought to mind the abortion I had at that time."

The woman, who was in her early fifties, had been struggling with thoughts of death since her late teen years but had never made the connection. Only the Holy Spirit could make the connection and set her free.

Similarly, one evening I was working with a young woman who had asked to be discipled. As we looked at 1 John 2:12–14, the Lord revealed to her from His Word that she was a spiritual baby. She said, "I am clearly a spiritual baby because I am weak, being overcome by the enemy in many areas of my life, and the Word of God does not abide in me on a consistent basis." Notice that she made her evaluation based on the truth of God's Word and not on her own assumptions.

As we explored how she was being overcome, I took her to Genesis 3 and she methodically observed the text. While we were examining the emotions of shame and guilt, she began to cry. I asked her what the Lord had brought to mind as we were in His Word, and she stated, "I have never told anyone this before, and no one knows this about me, but . . ." She hesitated to try to gain some measure of composure, and with tears streaming down her face she continued, "I have a lot of guilt and shame because I look at pornography and I sometimes masturbate." I asked her if the pornography involved looking at women or men. She said, "Both," and then confessed, "but mainly women." When I asked her when this entered her life she stated, "I have no idea." I responded by telling her that I knew she did not know and then asked her to pray and ask the Spirit of truth to lead her to the truth.

After she prayed, she hesitated and said, "What came to mind does not make sense." When I asked her what the Lord had brought to her mind, she said, "A memory that doesn't make sense." I asked her if she would share her memory. She began to recall a time in her later elementary years when she and her cousin were playing in a room and they began to "explore" with one another. She said this had happened on several occasions. I asked her if the cousin was a girl or a boy. She said, "A girl." Weeping, she confessed her shame but then quickly added, "But we were just kids, and that's what kids do." I then stated, "Then why the guilt and tears?" I asked her what she thought the Lord would think of the behavior. She said, "I honestly have no clue." I asked her to ask Him. So she bowed her head and asked the Lord. Immediately she looked up and said, "Now I am really confused because only one word came to my mind." I asked her what word the Lord had brought to mind, and she said, "Abomination," and then added, "I have no idea what that means." Immediately, the Lord brought to my mind

Leviticus 18:22 and Romans 1:26–27. As I showed her in His Word what the Lord calls an abomination, she wept.

It might interest you to know how the Lord had her surrender her will to His will and what He impressed her to do in obedience. She immediately confessed her sin to the Lord. As she was praying, the Lord instructed her to contact her cousin and ask for forgiveness. Although humiliating and difficult, she obeyed what she sensed the Lord was directing her to do. It may also be of interest to know that since she obeyed, she has not struggled with pornography or masturbation. Today she walks in freedom from a sin that overwhelmed her life with guilt and shame. Praise the Savior and Deliverer of our souls!

Step Five: Faith: A Surrendered Will and Obedience to His Word

Once the sin has been exposed by the Lord, it is time to search the Word for the solution. The following story is taken from my dissertation and serves as an excellent illustration of this step. As I share LeAnn's story, look for the specific ways the Lord used His Word to guide her to spiritual healing. Also look for LeAnn's response in faith, which is evidenced by the personal surrender of her will and obedience to God's Word.

LeAnn's Story

LeAnn first came for help because she was having frequent and debilitating panic attacks and she had witnessed the transformation of two of her friends. During the first meeting, LeAnn stated, "I have heard that at some point in this process I will have to go to people and ask for their forgiveness." LeAnn was aware of this process because a couple of women had already asked her for forgiveness for past offenses. She was intrigued with the changes in the lives of these women. She was overwhelmed by fear and anxiety. As she prayed and asked the Lord for His perspective, He immediately brought to her mind a woman's name. A previous conflict with this woman in the church and a scandal involving the woman's husband also plagued her mind. The humiliating and public sin was biblically handled when the pastor exercised church discipline according to Matthew 18:15–17. However, the incident resulted in hurt feelings and in a residual conflict between LeAnn and the woman because of LeAnn's sins of gossip and slander.

As LeAnn prayed, one thing became very evident: this would be LeAnn's first step of personal surrender and act of obedience. LeAnn would go no further in the discipleship process until the conflict was resolved.

One recurring theme throughout Scripture that also bears true in the discipleship process is that every act of personal surrender and obedience is followed by a subsequent revelation or unveiling of Christ. Also bearing witness to this truth, Jesus states, "He who has My commandments and keeps them, he it is who loves Me; and he who loves Me shall be loved by My Father, and I will love him, and will **disclose Myself** to him" (John 14:21, emphasis added).

Similarly, when an individual refuses to surrender his or her will and obey the Lord, a veiling occurs. One cannot proceed to go forward in the discipleship process when there is a refusal to obey what the Holy Spirit has revealed. In fact, Scripture states, "But prove yourselves doers of the Word, and not merely hearers who **delude themselves**" (James 1:22, emphasis added).

The Lord used Jeremiah 1:10 to allow LeAnn to see that she had some things in her life that He wanted to pluck up and destroy. Initially, this was all that LeAnn could see; however, she would later discover that this process was necessary for Him to be able to build and plant.

LeAnn was taken in Scripture to Matthew 5:23–24, where the Lord teaches the importance of leaving one's offering before the altar and reconciling with one's brother or sister before presenting the offering to Him. She knew immediately the Lord was leading her to reconcile with her sister in Christ. LeAnn tearfully admitted that she had played a part in the conflict because she had talked about the incident to others. Basically, LeAnn owned her part in the sin between the two women. When LeAnn realized her sin had not only separated the fellowship between her and her sister in Christ but also altered her fellowship with the Lord, she was devastated. With tears streaming down her face, she resolved in her heart to confess her sin to the Lord and ask for His forgiveness first and then ask the woman for forgiveness as well. LeAnn realized that for her to make things right with Him, she had to make things right with her former friend. Additionally, LeAnn allowed the Holy Spirit to bring other people to mind whom she had involved in the conflict with her words. When LeAnn left that day, she knew the Lord had revealed truth to her and that she was going to need His strength to obey.

LeAnn's effort to get in touch with the woman was met with opposition. However, the Lord had a plan, and LeAnn began to seek out the other people involved as the Holy Spirit revealed truth. When the last person was contacted, which happened to be the pastor of the church, LeAnn finally was able to meet with the woman and later her husband to ask for their forgiveness for the gossip and slander. LeAnn recalls, "I remember driving to her house and thinking, 'This is between You and me, Lord. I am doing this out of obedience to You.'" The woman was overwhelmed with LeAnn's obedience and forgave her immediately. The fact that LeAnn had gone to others first, especially the pastor, caused the woman to be humbled greatly, and their relationship was immediately restored. LeAnn then knew the reason for the delay in reaching her first. Further, she realized the Lord was in control of this discipleship process. LeAnn remembers feeling as if the weight of the world had just left her. The reconciliation had occurred on a Friday. She recalls, "That first Sunday, following the reconciliation, we were told we would be celebrating the Lord's Supper that evening. I knew I could partake of it freely without any guilt. It was the sweetest Lord's Supper ever." Little did LeAnn realize that this act of obedience would have a domino effect, and it would serve as a catalyst for her complete healing in the subsequent months.

After LeAnn had surrendered her will and obeyed, she was ready to proceed in the discipleship process. The Lord used 1 John 2:12–14 to help her understand that she was in process and that she was a spiritual baby. However, He used 1 John 2:12–14 to show LeAnn that she did not have to remain a spiritual baby. LeAnn began to long for spiritual growth. The Lord began to place a hunger in her heart for the Word of God. Upon realizing the Word of God did not abide in her, LeAnn began regularly to attend and participate in Bible study.

I spoke to LeAnn the other day and asked about her panic attacks. She smiled and said, "I don't have them anymore. In fact, I haven't had one since the day I surrendered and obeyed the Lord ten years ago."

Step Six: Pray to Identify the Connecting Voice

In this part of the process, it is vital that you connect the voice with the sin and emotion. This step in the process is extremely important when you consider the role the mind plays in regard to the heart. Remember, what you think will affect what you do and how you feel.

As you have seen by now, oftentimes we attribute God's voice to thoughts that do not align with the truth of His Word. The most helpful way to identify the voice is to simply allow the Holy Spirit to bring up the thoughts you have been suppressing. This can be a frightening experience for some who have spent years pushing the thoughts down or trying to avoid them altogether.

Consider the following examples of two women who traced the thoughts in their heads to the wrong voice.

Ava's Story

Ava came for help with severe depression and anxiety. With a master's degree in psychology, Ava had learned to medicate her emotions and modify her behavior to cope. By the time we met, she was unable to cope any longer.

I remember distinctly the impact Genesis 3 had on her. As she worked through the passages, she began to see the connection between her emotions and sin. Initially, she spent her time and energy blaming her parents for all her pain. But as she began to consider her own responses, which were not without sin, she began to allow the Holy Spirit to deal with her. When I asked her if she struggled with the emotion of shame, she stated, "I don't think so." I instructed her to ask the Lord. After she prayed, she looked up and said, "I think I do." I instructed her to go home and ask the Spirit of truth to lead her to all the shameful thoughts in her mind. I told her to list the thoughts on one side of the paper and then let me know when she was finished. She emailed me two days later and said, "Wow! I had no idea how much shame I had in my heart. I am shocked because I have listed 156 shameful thoughts that I guess I have suppressed."

The next instruction involves the use of a Bible concordance. I told her to examine the words *ashamed* and *shame* by looking up every reference in Scripture and listing the facts to hear God's voice on the subject.

After she had discovered God's voice, I instructed her to take every thought that the Holy Spirit had brought to mind and weigh it against the Word of God. Then I instructed her to ask the Lord if there was anything she needed to surrender her will to and any act of obedience to follow.

Jenna's Story

Similarly, I have been working with my daughter in regard to fear. Jenna has invested much time asking the Lord to reveal anything she is hiding, covering, or blaming others for in regard to fear. Through her teachable spirit and tender heart, the Lord revealed several roots of sin that had been covered or hidden, or that she had blamed others for. As she systematically surrendered her will to His Word and obeyed His instruction regarding each sin, she experienced a measure of freedom in regard to fear.

However, a life-changing event would prove to be the "bump" necessary for any residual fear to resurface, and this time it resurfaced with a vengeance. Having surrendered to full-time missions years before, she and her husband sensed it was time to uproot everything and move their family twelve hours from home for seminary training. This act of obedience was quite costly. They were willing to leave family, a new home, and a great job to obey the Lord. The most costly of all involved moving my two grandsons: Andrew, who was two years four months, and Luke, who was only four months old at the time. (They were born on the exact same day two years apart. The grandmother in me thought you might need to know that!)

As soon as the decision was made, my daughter began to have physical symptoms that involved a "heavy sensation in the right side of her head." After numerous tests and a frightening trip to the ER, the doctor explained that the test results were all negative. It was wonderful news, and we were all thankful. But as the symptoms persisted, and she and her husband prayed, they both sensed this was a spiritual battle.

After the move, the symptoms seemed to escalate, and so did Jenna's fear. After prayerful consideration, I asked Jenna if she would be willing to list her thoughts of fear on paper. I will never forget the look of sheer terror on her face as she wept and trembled at the thought. I sensed the Lord might be directing Jenna to bring the thoughts that she had suppressed for years up to the surface so He could expose the lies to the truth.

Hesitantly, she agreed to ask the Holy Spirit to lead her to the truth by exposing the thoughts of fear in her head. She called me the next day after having spent several hours listening to the Lord and writing down her thoughts. This is where the blank legal pad comes into play. She said, "Mom, you will never believe this, and I am embarrassed to say this, but I have listed 125 thoughts!" I remember telling Jenna that this only verified the magnitude of the stronghold that fear had on her life.

As she was able to objectively look at the thoughts on paper, the Lord showed her they could all be placed in two categories: doubt (or unbelief) and death. She confessed that some of her thoughts were against the Lord and His Word, which seemed to trouble her most. Looking at the two categories, she could easily trace the thoughts to the source and the enemy's voice because none of them lined up with Scripture.

Once the thoughts were exposed, I encouraged her to do a word study on the words *fear* and *afraid*, using a Bible concordance. Jenna spent hours looking at every reference from Genesis to Revelation. She would call me and tell me with excitement what the Lord showed her in His Word regarding fear. As Jenna placed God's Word (voice) next to the thoughts in her head, which she discovered were from the enemy, she began to see truth. She began to see how listening to the wrong voice had affected her life and held her captive to fear for years. She saw that the thoughts of fear had controlled what she did and how she felt. She also learned that God's Word was the only reliable voice of truth! As she continues to surrender her will and obey the voice of the Lord, she walks in the freedom from fear! Praise the Emancipator of our souls!

I have learned that we do not recognize the source of the voice in our heads. We do not realize the serpent is still speaking (Gen. 3:1). I have also learned that we engage in a conversation with the enemy (Gen. 3:2). We do this when we meditate on and rehearse in our minds the deceptive thoughts. I have also learned that it is just a matter of time before we act on the thoughts and are controlled by the emotional baggage they leave behind.

Now that we have considered he is still speaking today, we need to examine how we allow his voice to enter.

How Does the Voice of the Enemy Enter?

Satan is the master of deception. His goal is to "steal, and kill, and destroy" (John 10:10). The last thing the enemy wants is for you to identify his voice. Therefore, he will deceive you into thinking the thoughts you are having originate within you. It is also important for you to remember that Satan is not your only enemy.

Let's look in Scripture and identify our three enemies as believers.

1. Answer the following questions using Ephesians 2:1–3.

   a. What state or condition were you in before salvation according to verse 1?

   _____

   b. What course were you formerly walking or living before salvation according to verses 2–3?

   1) _____

   2) _____

   3) _____

   c. What did this lifestyle look like according to verses 2–3?

   1) _____ (v. 2)

   (Hint) What do you think the "sons of disobedience" are doing?

2) Indulge the desires of the _____ (v. 3)

3) Indulge the desires of the _____ (v. 3)

It may interest you to know that the word "mind" is the Greek word *dianoia*, which means "understanding, intellectual faculty, **thoughts**, and **imaginations**" (emphasis added).[50]

2. Do you think it is possible for the world and our flesh to become entry points for the enemy to build a stronghold in our minds? _____

3. What are some of the ways the world and the flesh can be entry points for the enemy in the life of a believer?

_____

_____

4. Now look at Proverbs 4:20–23 and answer the following questions.

a. What is the clear instruction given to the son in verse 20? _____

_____

_____

b. Where is the son instructed to keep the Word according to verse 21?

1) _____

2) _____

c. What is the benefit of keeping the Word of the Lord according to verse 22?

1) _____

2) _____

d. What is the son instructed to "watch over" in verse 23? _____
For review purposes, what is your heart? _____ ,
_____ and _____ .

e. In what manner is the son instructed to watch over his heart according to verse 23? "With all _____."

f. Why is the son instructed to watch over his heart according to verse 23?

_____

5. How do the instructions given in Proverbs 4 tie in with the believer's three enemies in Ephesians 2?

_____

Are you guarding what you allow in your mind with all diligence?

a. What specific things have you been indulging in that are clearly from the world? Ask the Spirit of truth to lead you.

b. What specific things have you been indulging in that are clearly from the flesh?

Remember to ask the Spirit of truth to lead you. If you knew the answer, you would not need help in this area.

6. Now look at 1 Peter 2:11 and answer the following questions.

a. What does Peter instruct his fellow brothers in Christ to do?

b. What specifically do these fleshly lusts do to us?

Did you realize that every time you indulge in fleshly lusts, you are actually waging war against your own soul/heart?

Do you see the correlation between your enemies and the need to guard your heart?

Consider the following information regarding the believer's three enemies.

SPIRITUAL ENEMIES: EPHESIANS 2:1–3

The apostle Paul reminds the church in Ephesus that they have three enemies: the world, the flesh, and the devil (Eph. 2:1–3). Interestingly, the Word of God gives the church instructions on how to deal precisely with each enemy.

1. For example, Romans 12:1–2 states, "Present your bodies a living and holy sacrifice, acceptable to God, which is your spiritual service of worship. And do not be conformed to this world, but be transformed by the **renewing of your mind**" (emphasis added).

2. The apostle John states, "For whatever is born of God overcomes the world; and this is the victory that has **overcome the world**—our faith" (1 John 5:4, emphasis added).

3. When the enemy is the flesh, Galatians 5:24 tells us how to deal with it: "Now those who belong to Christ Jesus have **crucified the flesh** with its passions and desires" (emphasis added).

4. The way to combat Satan is found in James 4:7: "**Submit therefore to God**. Resist the devil and he will flee from you" (emphasis added). Note the order. First, one must submit to God. When this submission occurs, the devil is resisted and then he flees.

Strikingly, the Lord is saying essentially the same thing with every enemy. Renewing one's mind, overcoming the world, crucifying the flesh, and submitting to God can all be summed up when a personal surrender of the will and obedience to God's Word is present. Remarkably, this definition is one of faith. Similarly, all these actions involve the choice of the believer. Which enemy are you encountering? What would the Lord have you do?

WHAT ABOUT YOU?

"So then, my beloved, just as you have always obeyed . . . work out your salvation with fear and trembling; for it is God who is at work in you, both to will and to work for His good pleasure" (Phil. 2:12–13).

1. You may want to stop and do this now. Get a blank legal pad. Prayerfully ask the Lord to reveal to you the thoughts that have consumed you in regard to fear. Listen and write down the thoughts that come to mind. You may be afraid or embarrassed to admit some of the thoughts. No matter how difficult it is for you, write them down.

2. Now, look at the thoughts that have surfaced. Take each thought and look at it in light of the truth of God's Word. If this thought does not align with God's Word, it just may be the voice of the enemy speaking to you.

3. Now look at each thought. Consider the following two questions:

   a. Does this thought cast doubt on God's Word?

   b. Does this thought cast doubt on God's character?

   c. If the answer is yes to either question, look in Scripture (you may need to use the help of a concordance) and write the truth next to the thought (lie).

4. Now, ask the Lord if there is anything you need to surrender your will to or obey in regard to this thought. This is what it looks like to take "every thought captive to the obedience of Christ" (2 Cor. 10:5).

HOW TO BEGIN?

The best place to begin is with a blank legal pad. Prayerfully ask the Holy Spirit to help bring to your mind the thoughts that are controlling your mind. Let Him bring the thoughts of fear, shame, guilt, and anger to the surface. Write your thoughts down as they come. This will be difficult. The thoughts that are deep within are embarrassing, are hurtful, and have been hidden or suppressed for years. However, they are deep within, and they are affecting what you are doing and how you feel.

When you have brought the thought to the light, place it against the truth of God's Word. You will see that it does not align with truth. Hebrews 11:6 states, "Without faith it is impossible to please [God]." These thoughts have not been pleasing to God, and they have dictated the way you have responded and felt for far too long. Remember, biblical faith must have three components:

1. Firm conviction of God's Word (His voice)—God's Spirit using the Word

2. Personal surrender of your will to His will (His Word)

3. Obedience to His Word

Now that you have allowed the Spirit of truth to reveal your hidden thoughts and you have brought them against the truth of God's Word, you will see and agree that they do not line up with truth. This is the first step toward a biblical faith. But until you surrender your will to God's will and walk in the obedience of His Word to what He has revealed, you have not exercised faith. Remember, the goal is to please the Lord! Faith pleases Him!

Look at the thoughts one by one and ask the Lord what He would have you surrender your will to and obey in regard to each specific thought. He will show you what it is attached to in your life. Let me caution you at this point. Do not disregard any thought He may bring to your mind as an act of obedience, no matter how trivial or difficult the act of surrender and obedience may be. He is the One leading to truth. He alone can set you free! Simply surrender your will and walk in obedience to what He shows you in regard to each thought. Remember, whatever He reveals will align with His Word! Typically, I will place the act of surrender and obedience next to the thought listed. Once I have obeyed, it is no longer an issue or struggle. In essence, it is gone. This does not mean that it is gone for good. Unfortunately, we are not glorified yet.

However, when the thoughts and struggles resurface, I am equipped with what to do.

As you surrender your will to God's will and walk in obedience of His Word, allowing each thought that has held you captive to be taken captive to the obedience of Christ, you will begin to walk in freedom. With every act of obedience, you can expect more truth to be illumined. This is a process. Remember, prayer is a command and therefore an act of surrender and obedience. More than likely, you will not receive two or three acts to surrender and obey. Oftentimes, people want to know everything all at once. This can be frustrating. Do the one thing He has placed before you. You will learn that after you have surrendered your will and walked in obedience, He will lead you to the next thing. You will begin to walk in the freedom that Christ alone can give. This is what Paul meant when he said, "Walk by the Spirit, and you will not carry out the desire of the flesh" (Gal. 5:16).

Always remember, He will not ask you to surrender your will or obey more than He did!

NOTES

CHAPTER 8

IMPROPER WAYS TO DEAL WITH THE VOICES IN OUR HEADS

"Woe to those who go down to Egypt [the world] for help."
(Isaiah 31:1a)

Now that we have considered how to recognize the voice of the enemy and how it enters, we need to consider the improper ways believers have chosen to deal with the voices. For the purpose of this workbook, I would like to address two coping mechanisms that are becoming more and more widely infused in the church today: medication and behavior modification.

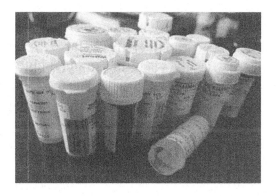

MEDICATING OUR EMOTIONS

Consider the following stories. Remember, the stories are true, but the names have been changed to protect the identities of the counselees.

Jennifer's Story

I remember distinctly the conversation that took place at Jennifer's house while I shared what the Lord had revealed to me from Genesis 3. We were discussing her daughter Carrie's catatonic state because of the numerous psychotropic drugs she was taking to treat her depression, anxiety, and the "voices in her head." The psychiatrist had agreed to begin tapering off Carrie's medication because of the posturing that had developed as a side effect of Carrie's medication. Posturing is a condition that can occur when a person is overmedicated, resulting in an involuntary flexion or extension of the arms or legs. We walked through Genesis 3 as it pertains to the heart, and Jennifer began to question the decision to medicate her daughter. I explained the various emotions that resulted from the sin in one's life and our tendency to treat the emotions rather than biblically deal with the sin. At one point, Jennifer protested, stating that the medication had helped stop the voices in Carrie's head. One can only imagine the silence in the room when Carrie spoke up and stated, "The voices have never stopped." Shocked and surprised by Carrie's statement, Jennifer said, "But Carrie, you stopped talking about the voices, so I assumed they were gone." At that moment, I realized that the medication had not silenced the voices; rather, it had only served to silence Carrie. In truth, the medication had provided a sort of prison for allowing the voices to continue for many years.

Anna's Story

Further insight was gleaned when Anna came to my house for biblical counseling after a failed attempt at suicide. Anna presented with depression, anxiety, and fear and had tried to take her life by ingesting approximately forty pills of Valium to (in her words) "silence the screaming voices in my head." Instead of taking her life, the drug kept her awake for over three days and nights. The only adverse side effect she reported was a numbing in her throat for days.

At the first meeting, with tears in her eyes, Anna grabbed her head with her hands and stated, "The voices are screaming in my head, and I cannot stop them." After prayer asking the Spirit of truth to lead us to the truth, Anna and I began to examine Genesis 3 in light of the heart of man. I explained to Anna that the enemy targets the mind specifically and that he is still speaking today. Anna confessed that she had been on antidepressants since her parents put her on them at the age of fifteen. She was fifty years old at the time of our meeting. For thirty-five years she had been medicating the emotions that were the result of things in her life she had spent years covering, hiding, and blaming everyone around her for.

One of the most enlightening moments with Anna came when she returned two weeks later for her second meeting. She began our time together stating that after she left my house, she took herself off all the medications she had been on for thirty-five years. The nurse in me panicked as I asked her why she had done this, since I had not instructed nor would ever recommend that she do so. I will never forget what she told me: "I prayed when I got home and I sensed the Lord directing me to stop immediately. If the enemy was targeting my mind, then it made sense for me to stop so that I could think clearly with my mind. I did not take another pill and have continued not to take them for the past two weeks." With my mouth wide open (literally), I asked, "Are you okay?" She said, "Oh yes. Immediately I noticed that the voices in my head have not stopped, but they are not screaming at me." As she was speaking, Galatians 5:19 came to my mind: "Now the deeds of the flesh are evident . . ." Anna read the list of the deeds of the flesh, which include the word "sorcery" (Gal. 5:19–21). I explained to her that the Greek word for "sorcery" is *pharmakeia*, which means a "drug used both for curative and medicinal purposes."[51] In essence, the drugs were actually "feeding" the voice of the enemy that had been screaming in her head for months.

As Anna began to walk in obedience to God's Word, she reported, "The voices in my head are gone. My mind is at peace now. It feels wonderful!" Although Anna experienced relief, she knows that the voices that once plagued her may attempt to come back. She has found she is most vulnerable when she is not in God's Word consistently or when she has not obeyed His voice (Word). She has learned to take the legal pad out and write down the thoughts in her head. She knows that every "voice" or thought that does not align with God's Word is not truth. She is able to identify the voice, and she refuses to allow it to guide her choices and affect her emotions. She is learning to hear His voice and follow Him (John 10:27).

One thing that I must clarify is that I am not anti-physicians or anti-medications. I come from a family of medical professionals. My own daughter is a physician, my sister is a nursing instructor, and I am a former registered nurse. However, what I have learned from the Counselor and His Word is that **if sin is the underlying issue, medication is not the answer!**

BEHAVIOR MODIFICATION

Sadly, and all too often, we focus on the behavior of an individual. When you think about the heart as one's mind, will, and emotions, you must consider that the will is not the target area. The target area is the mind! In his book *Shepherding a Child's Heart*, pastor and author Tedd Tripp discusses the topic of biblical child-rearing. I learned, after reading Tripp's book, that the behavior is never the issue; rather, it is the heart. Tripp states, "The central focus of parenting is the gospel. You need to direct not simply the behavior of your children, but the attitudes of their hearts."[52] This is true with spiritual children as well. According to Tripp, "It is the Holy Spirit's task to work through the Word of God to change their hearts. Even when the Spirit illuminates and quickens them to life, it is a life of progressive growth."[53] The same is true with discipleship.

I have counseled many women who attempt to cover their emotions by immersing themselves in church activities and ministries. (But this is not true of women only.) I am beginning to see an influx of women whose husbands are steeped in pornography. At present, I am counseling a woman who is in the process of a legal separation because of the husband's addiction to pornography. He has been unfaithful during their entire marriage. Sadly, the husband has been in seminary the whole time, thinking that having a godly wife or attending a seminary would cure him. Despite several attempts at utilizing various behavior modifications, such as Covenant Eyes and accountability partners, the man is worse than ever. In fact, all the behavior modifications proved to be the means he used to conceal his sin while it continued to fester and grow.

Please do not misunderstand me. I am in no way criticizing Covenant Eyes or the need for accountability, but when this is the given solution, I do not agree. Jesus clearly taught, "That which proceeds out of the man, that is what defiles the man. For **from within, out of the heart of men, proceed** the evil thoughts, fornications, thefts, murders, adulteries, deeds of coveting and wickedness, as well as deceit, sensuality, envy, slander, pride and foolishness" (Mark 7:20–22, emphasis added). According to Jesus, the issue is a heart issue. No amount of behavior modification can heal a sick heart. Again, **if sin is the underlying issue, behavior modification is not the answer!**

WHAT DO THE SCRIPTURES SAY?

Do the Scriptures offer the church an answer? Do they provide an adequate cure? Can the God who created the human heart also sustain and heal the heart? Paul addresses the issue by using the analogy of the "war" within our minds, which causes the "lofty" thoughts to become greater than the knowledge of God. Let's take some time to look at a couple of great cross-references to the biblical framework established in Genesis 3. We will be dissecting 2 Corinthians 10:3–5 and James 4:7. Answer the following questions using the following cross-references:

2 Corinthians 10:3–5

1. What does Paul liken our "walk in the flesh" to according to verse 3? _____

   Remember, Paul is speaking to a church. These are believers who have been justified and are in the process of sanctification. Therefore, Paul likens sanctification to WAR!

2. If this is not a fleshly war, what type of warfare is Paul describing? _____

3. Now, list the facts about the weapons we have been given for this war in verse 4.

   a. They are not of the _____ ; therefore, they are _____ .

   b. They are divinely _____ .

   c. They are for the _____ of _____ .

   Did you notice that the weapons are not meant to merely help us cope? They have the power to destroy!

   Note: The word *stronghold* or *fortress* is the Greek word *ochuroma*. According to John MacArthur, "*ouchuroma* was used in extrabiblical Greek to refer to a prison. People under siege in a fortress were imprisoned there by the attacking forces. The word is also used to refer to a tomb."[54]

4. Verse 5 describes the enemy's strategy in this war and what he opposes.

   a. The Strategy: _____ and raised up against _____ _____ things

   b. Who is doing the destroying in verse 5? _____

   (Oftentimes, we want the Lord to do this for us.)

   Note: It might interest you to know that the word "speculations" in verse 5 is the Greek word *logismos*, which means "considerations and intentions which are hostile to the gospel."[55] Speculations are thoughts that imprison our minds.

   c. Do you have thoughts that imprison your mind? Ask the Holy Spirit to lead you to truth in this area, and write down what He brings to mind.

d. Where is the "knowledge of God" found? _____

5. Now, look at Ephesians 6:17. What exactly is the sword of the Spirit? _____

   Note: The sword of the Spirit and prayer are the believer's only offensive weapons (Eph. 6:17-18).

   Considering 2 Corinthians 10:5 and Ephesians 6:17, what is the weapon of our warfare?

   _____ Remember, this weapon is divinely powerful for the destruction of fortresses. Like any other weapon, it is only effective as we wield it. So how do we wield it?

6. What are we instructed to do in 2 Corinthians 10:5? _____

7. How obedient was Christ? Look at Philippians 2:8 to answer the question.

Think about it. The speculations, or thoughts that imprison our minds, are elevated and lofty. They are so high they supersede the Word of God (knowledge of God). However, when we wield our sword, by surrendering our wills and walking in obedience to His Word, the fortress is destroyed. Notice we are the ones doing this.

Oftentimes, I hear people say, "I keep praying and asking the Lord to take this away." I always follow this statement by saying, "Are you doing your part?" Our victory over the enemy is a finished and completed work accomplished by Christ on the cross. However, we must respond in faith to what His Word declares for us to experience the victory personally.

James 4:7

1. Now let's look at another passage that deals with the enemy. Read James 4:7 and list the verse in the order it is written:

   a. _____ to God.

   b. _____ the devil.

   c. He (the devil) will _____.

2. Do you think the order is important? What does it mean to submit to God? _____

We so often focus on resisting the devil. There are books written where the focus has been placed on the enemy. But if we would take notice of the order of God's Word and obey Him by submitting to Him, we would realize the enemy is resisted, and therefore he must flee. In other words, by placing the focus on the Lord and submitting (personal surrender and obedience) to His Word, we will find that this is **how the enemy is resisted!** We will also soon realize he has had to flee and whatever has been the issue will not be the issue anymore (or at least until he attempts to come back).

What About You?

1. What are the speculations and lofty things in your mind?

2. How have these things raised themselves up against the knowledge of God in your life?

3. What have you refused to submit (surrender your will and obey) to God?

Ask the Holy Spirit to lead you to the root of the issue, and then be willing to surrender your will to what He reveals and walk in obedience to His Word regarding the sin. Once you have obeyed completely, the fortress will be destroyed! What is He "putting His finger on" in your life?

CHAPTER 9

THE WORD OF GOD ABIDES WITHIN

"Be diligent to present yourself approved to God as a workman who
does not need to be ashamed, handling accurately the word of truth."

(2 Tim. 2:15)

We have spent quite a bit of time looking at ways we can be deceived by the world, our flesh, and the enemy in the previous chapters. We have also looked at a biblical framework designed to evaluate our hearts and teach us how to overcome the enemy found in Genesis 3. However, to be thorough, and in an effort to deal with all areas of spiritual immaturity we discovered in 1 John 2:12–14, we must examine what it means to have the Word of God abide within us.

Many people are of the opinion that reading and studying the Bible is what it means to have the Word of God abide within us. Some will go even further and memorize the Word. And yet, that is still not the full definition of having the Word of God abide within us. Although these are excellent and necessary disciplines, the Word of God does not abide within us **until** we surrender our wills and obey what it says. In other words, there is a vast difference between me being in the Word and the Word being in me!

Think about it. When we read, study, and memorize the Word, we have merely received information. Only when we surrender our wills and obey the Word will transformation occur! Isn't that the goal? Look carefully at the Lord's instruction in regard to His Word in the Great Commission. In Matthew 28:19–20, Jesus says to His disciples, "Go therefore and make disciples of all the nations . . . teaching them to **observe all** that I commanded you" (emphasis added).

The word "observe" in Matthew 28:20 is the Greek word *tereo*, which means "to keep an eye on, to watch attentively"; figuratively, it means "to obey, to fulfill." It is used as a present active infinitive verb, which means that the subject is responsible to watch attentively and obey God's Word as a way of life.

I believe over the years the church has been responsible to teach what the Lord commands, but I fear we have fallen short of teaching others to obey. Jesus' words "teaching them to observe all that I commanded you" implies accountability and interaction with one another. In essence, this phrase is the embodiment of true discipleship.

Sadly, and too often, I find that the Word does not abide within the ladies I teach and counsel because many of them do not even know what the Word actually says. At times, I hear the Word misquoted. Most of the time, I hear it taken out of context. An important rule of Bible study is to keep the passage you are studying in context. Context is the setting in which the text lives, and it is significant when we are endeavoring to interpret the Word correctly.

MY TESTIMONY

For the first twenty-five years of my life as a believer in Christ, this was my testimony. I was raised in a denomination where the Word of God was not the focus. I never had a quiet time and actually had no clue what that even meant. My attempt at Bible reading would consist of the Psalms and Proverbs because they were the easiest to read and understand. The one psalm I would avoid at all cost was Psalm 119. After all, who could stay awake through 176 verses! I find this humorous now because Psalm 119 is actually my FAVORITE psalm—because the entire psalm is all about the Word of God!

Unfortunately, the Word of God was not even opened many times in the church in which I grew up. The pastor would read or sometimes just quote a verse and use it as a springboard for his topic of discussion that day. Sadly, I grew up thinking that when the Holy Spirit is really present in a service, the Word would not need to be preached. The Holy Spirit and His gifts were the main focus.

I was also taught that I could lose my salvation. I remember spending the majority of my teenage years asking "Jesus into my heart" over and over again. After all, I struggled with daily sin. I was taught that the Scripture teaches, "No one who abides in Him sins; no one who sins has seen Him or knows Him" (1 John 3:6). It was passages like this, taken out of context and not appropriately handled, that caused me great grief during the first twenty-five years of my life as a believer. It would be years later that I would learn that the word "sins" in 1 John 3:6 is in the present tense and that this meant that sin was the habit of one's life. I would also learn later that when the Scriptures describe sin in the life of a true follower of Christ, it is in the aorist tense. The aorist tense indicates a singular (or punctiliar) action as opposed to a continuous action (present tense). In other words, sin is not going to be the continuous habit of lifestyle for the believer. I also had no clue that there were three tenses to salvation and that sanctification was a process.

Little did I know growing up that the Spirit of God would use the Word of God to truly set me free from years of total ignorance and extreme frustration trying to live the Christian life. I remember many nights crying out to the Lord to save me. I remember thinking I must not be sincere or saying the words correctly, because whatever I was doing or saying, it was NOT sticking. I think the best description of me during my teenage years and early twenties could best be summed up in Ephesians 4:14. I was like the little child "tossed here and there by waves, and carried about by every wind of doctrine."

I remember the day in my early thirties when I cried out to the Lord in frustration and said, "I can't do this anymore. I can't live the Christian life." It was as if I put up a white flag in my mind and was waving it at the Lord in surrender. This turned out to be a really good thing. I had to learn that I could not do anything to save myself or live the Christian life. If I could have done it, Christ would not have had to come and die in my place. I learned quickly that it takes God to satisfy God! My job was to simply get out of the way and let Him do it through me. In other words, He would lead by His Spirit through His Word, and I would simply surrender my will and obey!

I remember being totally honest with the Lord during this time in my life and crying out in confession by telling Him that I did not have a desire for His Word. I guess I thought I was telling Him something He did not already know. (That is the danger of not knowing His Word!) I also remember praying, "If You want me to have a desire for Your Word, You are going to have to give it to me." I even asked for an "insatiable desire" for Him and His Word, because I never wanted to walk away satisfied and thinking I was finished. I realize now that the Spirit of God was praying for me, for these are the kind of requests that we do not ask in and of ourselves.

I also realized at that moment that I would need to put myself in a Bible study where I could learn to study God's Word. I did not have the first clue where to begin. I enrolled in a study called Bible Study Fellowship. At first, Bible study seemed mechanical. I would do my lesson, but there was no real connection with my everyday life until about six months later. I had just prayed and asked the Lord for wisdom about a situation my oldest daughter was experiencing. Not giving it another thought, I picked up my lesson to complete it, and lo and behold, the answer was in the passage I was studying! I had not gone looking for it. The answer just seemed to leap off the page. I remember saying out loud, "Is this how You speak to people? Is this how You do it?" I knew that day the Lord had used His Word to give me the answer for which I had previously prayed. I simply obeyed what He said in His Word and watched the Lord take care of my daughter in a way I could have never done or even imagined! It was that day that the Word of God became a "living and active" part of my life (Heb. 4:12)! It was that day the Spirit of God, in His kindness and mercy, guided me specifically to His truth! Since that day, I have never approached prayer or His Word in the same way. That was over thirty years ago.

WHAT ABOUT YOU?

Is His Word living and active in your life, or is it dead and dormant to you? Do you have a passion and hunger for His Word? Interestingly, I have witnessed that a deep hunger for the Word develops as the women I have counseled over the years have allowed the Lord to first pluck up and destroy the things from their pasts that do not align with His Word. If you will recall from the previous chapters, this is the biblical pattern established in Jeremiah 1:10 when His Word is given to "pluck up and to break down, to destroy and to overthrow," so that He can "build and . . . plant."

WHERE TO BEGIN?

The best time to start is now. The best place to start is here. If you do not have a passion and hunger for His Word, confess this to Him (He already knows). Pray and ask Him to give you a deep hunger and desire for His Word.

Next, put yourself in His Word! Spend some time now asking the Spirit of truth to lead you to the truth about your passion/hunger for His Word. Be honest and write down the thoughts He brings to mind. Remember, if your thoughts do not align with the truth of God's Word, they are not from Him.

Now write a prayer to the Lord in response to what He has shown you. Remember, "all things are open and laid bare to the eyes of Him with whom we have to do" (Heb. 4:13).

WHAT'S NEXT?

Now that the Lord has shown you where you are in regard to His Word, the next step is to get in His Word. At this juncture, it will prove helpful to begin to learn how to study His Word. Basically, there are two approaches to Bible study: the Deductive Method and the Inductive Method. The following illustration shows how they differ.

Inductive	Deductive
God speaks ↓	God speaks ↓
Word ↓	Word ↓
YOU ↓	Others ↓
Others	**YOU**

Look at the illustration of both methods above. What do you see?

Notice, in the Deductive Method, God speaks through His Word to someone else—for example, your pastor. Then your pastor (or another person) gives God's Word to you.

In the Inductive Method, God speaks through His Word directly to you, and then you can become equipped to give His Word to others.

There is nothing wrong with the Deductive Method as long as the person handling the Word of God has handled it correctly. However, there is a real danger when the Word of God is placed in the wrong hands. There are many today saying they have a "word from God." Yet the "word" they are giving does not line up with the truths found in the Bible. The same thing was happening in the apostle Paul's day. Paul, warning Timothy, stated, "And the things which you have heard from me in the presence of many witnesses, **these entrust to faithful men**, who will be able to teach others also" (2 Tim. 2:2, emphasis added).

Paul encouraged Timothy, stating, "Be diligent to present yourself approved to God as a workman who does not need to be ashamed, handling accurately the word of truth" (2 Tim. 2:15). Even a casual look at this verse should cause the reader to take notice and heed Paul's counsel.

Just a few things that immediately can be seen:

1. We are responsible and commanded to be diligent.

2. We are seeking God's approval.

3. We are called "workmen," so it will involve effort on our part.

4. We can be ashamed at the way in which we have handled God's Word.

5. There is an accurate way to handle the truth of God's Word, which automatically implies that there is an inaccurate way as well.

The purpose of this workbook is to introduce you to the Inductive Method of Study, which comprises three steps:[56]

> 1) Observation
> 2) Interpretation
> 3) Application

Each step in the method answers a specific question:[57]

1. Observation–   What does God/the text say?

2. Interpretation–   What does God/the text mean?

3. Application–   How does God's Word apply to me?

In the past, you may have been involved in "Bible studies" that begin with application. For example, some Bible studies are solely concerned with how the text applies to the student. Let me caution you: this is an inaccurate way to handle the Word of truth. The Word of God NEVER begins with us! The Word of God ALWAYS begins with God! HE IS THE AUTHOR!

Read and record 2 Peter 1:20–21.

_____

_____

_____

A word of caution!

You will want to avoid "Bible studies" where you meet with others who simply want to discuss what **they** think the Bible means. I call this approach the "What the Bible Means to Me" study. This type of study can be very dangerous! We can honestly make the Bible say anything we want it to say. It does not matter what we think the Bible says. All that truly matters is the Author's perspective. You will find that when you handle the Word of God accurately, there will be one meaning (interpretation), and yet there can be many applications. If you have observed and interpreted the text accurately, the personal application of the text will simply "fall out" of the text without much effort on your part as the Holy Spirit applies it to your personal life. The effort on your part will be in observing, interpreting, and doing what He has said.

At this point, I would be remiss not to mention Bible study groups such as Bible Study Fellowship and Community Bible Study. Similarity exists in the Inductive Study approach; however, a heavy reliance on questions, lecturers, and training from others occurs. As a former student and leader in the Bible Study Fellowship, I can assure you this study provided an excellent introductory means for Bible study. However, personal frustration ensued in the summer months when lessons and teaching were unavailable, and no one was asking the pertinent questions.[58] I will forever be indebted to Bible Study Fellowship for introducing me to the Word of God.

The Precept Bible Study Method closely aligns with the work in this workbook since much of the training in the Inductive Method is derived from this ministry.[59] However, differences occur in method and means of interpretation. For example, in the Precept Bible Study Method, you are taught to mark key words and phrases by using colored pencils and creating symbols for recognition of specific words, such as _God_, _Jesus_, the _Holy Spirit_, _faith_, _love_, and so forth. After you have adequately read and marked the passage, you are instructed to make lists of facts using the words from the text itself as part of the observation process in the study. Interpreting the passage is accomplished by the use of various word study books and Bible dictionaries, and by cross-referencing Scripture with Scripture. In the application portion of the study, you are asked personal questions in alignment with the passage being studied. The Precept method is devoted to keeping the passage in context. It has been a life-changing way for me to learn to study the Word. The Inductive Method has provided me with invaluable skills in learning how to handle the Word of God accurately (2 Tim. 2:15).

However, as invaluable a tool as the Precept Bible Study Method has been, the one drawback was my reliance on the ministry to produce materials, videos, and training. I was still relying on another person to ask pertinent questions regarding the text and pertaining to application. The goal is to learn to rely on the Holy Spirit as you are given the tools necessary to handle the Word of God accurately for yourself.

Read and record John 14:26. _____

_____

_____

_____

THE BUILT-IN TEACHER

Answer the following questions using John 14:26.

1. Who is speaking in this verse? _____

   To whom is He speaking? _____ 60

2. What does Jesus call the Holy Spirit in this verse? _____

   a. Who sent the Holy Spirit? _____

   b. In whose name is He sent? _____

      Do you see the Trinity is this verse? Just a neat observation!

3. In this verse, what two things does Jesus say that the Holy Spirit will do?

   a. _____

   b. _____

If the Holy Spirit taught the disciples and brought back to their remembrance all that He said, will He not also teach us and bring back to our remembrance the things in His Word?

Therefore, no matter which method of study you choose—whether it be Bible Study Fellowship, Community Bible Study, Precept Bible Study Method, or learning how to study for yourself—the important factor is that you GET IN THE WORD! Even more significantly, LET THE WORD OF GOD GET IN YOU!

If you would like to learn how to study for yourself, keep reading. Hopefully, when you finish this chapter, you will not only be introduced to the Inductive Method but also be given some tools to help you in this endeavor.

SUGGESTED TOOLS TO HELP WITH INTERPRETATION:

1. New American Standard Bible or English Standard Version Bible (In this workbook, I am using the NASB 1977.)

2. Legal pad

3. Word study / dictionary for Old and New Testament

   I personally use and recommend the following word studies and dictionaries because they are easy to use, they are relatively inexpensive, the numbers correspond with *Strong's Concordance*, and they supply helpful cross-references within the definitions.

   > Zodhiates, Spiros, *The Complete Word Study New Testament*, Chattanooga: AMG Pub., 1992.

   > Zodhiates, Spiros, *The Complete Word Study New Testament Dictionary*, Chattanooga: AMG Pub., 1992.

   > Zodhiates, Spiros, *The Complete Word Study Old Testament*, Chattanooga: AMG Pub., 1994.

   > Baker, Warren and Eugene Carpenter, *The Complete Word Study Dictionary Old Testament*, Chattanooga: AMG Pub., 2003.

   > W. E. Vine, *Vine's Expository Dictionary of Old and New Testament Words*, Grand Rapids: Revell, 1981.

COMPUTER LEXICAL AIDS

Here are a few suggestions if you would prefer to use your computer for word studies:

1. Lexicon-Concordance Online Bible: www.lexiconcordance.com

2. Bible Study Tools: www.biblestudytools.com

3. Blue Letter Bible: www.blueletterbible.org

4. Bible dictionary such as Zondervan or Holman (see Bible bookstore/Amazon).

5. Bible concordance such as Strong's (see Bible book store/Amazon).

6. Trustworthy commentaries—Oftentimes I am asked, "Who is trustworthy, and how can we know?" Great question. There are many commentaries from which to choose; however, all commentaries are not trustworthy. For a more academic approach, I will typically access either Southern Baptist Seminary or Southwestern Baptist Seminary (because these are the ones I am most familiar with personally) to see what the professors are recommending for their classes. If I want a reliable and an easy-to-read-and-understand commentary, I frequently recommend John MacArthur and his work. I will also look at the bibliography section of authors/books I trust for reliable

sources. You may want to ask your pastoral staff and elders for recommendations as well.

NOTE: Please do not feel obligated to go out and purchase all these books at once. I am merely providing a list of books and websites that may be helpful as you begin to learn how to study the Word for yourself. If you are feeling a bit overwhelmed, you may want to begin with just one book.

LET'S GET STARTED

At this point, I think it would be helpful to take a few verses in Scripture and walk you through the process of how to study on your own.

Let's begin with the passage in Luke 10:38–42. Normally, I would begin in the first chapter of Luke and proceed throughout the book to put these passages in context. However, the purpose of this workbook is to give you tools to help you study on your own, and for brevity's sake we will focus on just these verses using two tools: *The Complete Word Study New Testament* and *The Complete Word Study Dictionary*, each by Zodhiates. You may also access the websites provided in the Computer Lexical Aids section for help if you prefer.

1. Before you begin reading or studying the Word, pray and ask the Lord Jesus to open your mind "to understand the Scriptures" (Luke 24:45). As you seek the Lord through His Word, ask your built-in Teacher to teach and instruct you (John 14:26).

CONTEXT

A key point when interpreting Scripture is to let context rule the interpretation. Context is the setting in which the text lives. For example, if you are studying Luke 10, you would need to look at Luke 9 and Luke 10 "lives" in between these two chapters. Likewise, you would need to look at the entire book of Luke because Luke 10 "lives" in the Gospel of Luke.

2. The account you are about to study is not located in any other gospel. To help place Luke 10:38–42 in context and for brevity's sake, begin by reading Luke 10:25–37. Pay close attention to the answer given in Luke 10:27. How does the parable about the Samaritan demonstrate Luke 10:27?

3. Do you see any connection between Luke 10:27, the parable of the Samaritan, and the passage we are focusing on in Luke 10:38–42? If not, you may want to keep doing the lesson and then come back to this question to help place Luke 10:38–42 in context.

_____

_____

_____

_____

_____

OBSERVATION

Oftentimes, we hurry through observation. Observation is THE MOST IMPORTANT step in the Inductive Method. Think about it. If we do not know what God has said, we cannot interpret or apply it correctly. In essence, an accurate interpretation and application will hinge off a correct observation.

1. Now, let's focus on Luke 10:38–42 by reading the text first. As you read the text, remember that the first step in the Inductive Method is observation, which answers the question "What does God/the text say?"

I am going to introduce you to two ways you can observe the text. In the first approach to observation, we will look at simply locating the subject of the text and listing the facts from the Scripture passage under the subject. The second approach we will examine will include diagramming the entire text of study.

LOCATE THE SUBJECT AND LIST THE FACTS

Now that you have read Luke 10:38–42, you probably noticed three key people in the story: Jesus, Martha, and Mary. You will want to divide your paper into the following three sections, each representing the subjects in the story. For the purpose of using this workbook, list the facts here (using the words from the text) under each name. For example,

Jesus

v. 38–was traveling with disciples

v. 41–

Martha

v. 38–welcomed Jesus into her home

v. 39 –

v. 40 –

Mary

v. 39 –

You may ask, "What if the text you are studying is not about a person?" Good question. In this case, you will want to read the text you are studying and simply locate the subject of the text. For example, if the word *faith* is the subject of the text you are studying, you will list facts from the text about faith under the word *faith*.

Sometimes the subject can be an entire phrase. For example, in 1 John 3, there is a comparison made between the "children of God" and the "children of the devil." These phrases will become the topics or subjects, and you will list the facts about each from the text under each of the subjects.

For example, look at the following illustration from 1 John 3:8–10.

Children of God	Children of the devil
v. 9 born of God	v. 8 practices sin
v. 9 does not practice sin	v. 10 does not practice righteousness
v. 9 His seed abides in him	v. 10 does not love his brother

At times, the Scriptures will make a comparison. You will want to look for and make note of words that compare, such as *like* or *as*. For example, in John 10, believers are compared to sheep. Similarly, Jesus is compared to a shepherd and calls Himself the "good shepherd." In the passage you will want to note the comparisons made by listing them under the subject "sheep" or "shepherd" and listing the facts about each under the subject.

DIAGRAMMING THE TEXT

Now I want to show you another option. I am going to diagram these sentences and include every word from the text using the NASB. I actually prefer this way when I am observing the text for myself, because I can see more detail.

When diagramming the sentences, typically the subject is a noun and the facts are the verbs, which follow the noun. Usually the prepositional phrases modify or answer questions about the subject and/or verbs.

The word *and* usually begins the list of facts, and the word *but* becomes the contrast. I typically will place the contrasts either directly under the subject contrasted or to the side of it. In this way, the information becomes a visual for me (since I am a visual learner).

In other words, the visual on the page will be

Not this   BUT   This

Study the following diagram as an example of how to diagram a passage.

Luke 10:38–42

v. 38 Now as they were traveling along,
    He (Who?)

    entered a certain village (What?)
    and
    a woman named **Martha** (Who?)

    welcomed Him (What?)
    into her home (Where?)
v. 39   and
    she had a sister
        called **Mary**

        was listening
        to the Lord's word
        seated at His feet
v. 40   **BUT**

        Martha

        was distracted
        with all her preparations
        and
        came up to **Him**
        and
        said, "Lord, do You not care
            that **my sister**
                has left me
                    to do all the serving alone?"

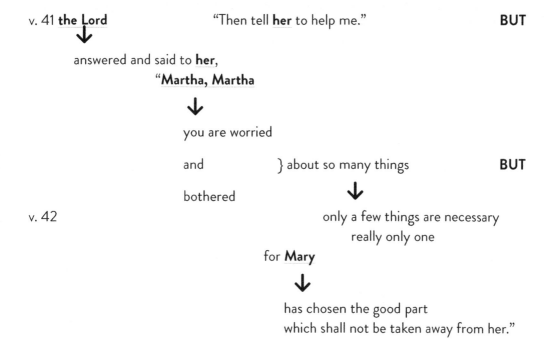

v. 41 **the Lord**   "Then tell **her** to help me."   **BUT**

answered and said to **her**,
       "**Martha, Martha**

       you are worried

       and   } about so many things   **BUT**

       bothered

v. 42   only a few things are necessary
       really only one

       for **Mary**

       has chosen the good part
       which shall not be taken away from her."

Did you notice that when you take the time to diagram the words from the text, the facts about Jesus, Martha, and Mary become quite visible? This step takes time, but I have found that it is time well spent. (It is important when you begin to study the Scriptures that you examine only a few verses at a time so that you will not become overwhelmed or get discouraged. It is far better to look intensely at one or two verses a day in your quiet time than to read an entire chapter and forget what you read.)

Did you also notice that you could simply use a legal pad to do either method of observation? In other words, you do not have to purchase a workbook to study a passage of Scripture. Amazing!

2. Now, using the diagramming method, look at the facts under each subject. Notice that they answer the question of either **who, what, when, where, why,** or **how.** To accurately examine the subject, you will need to interrogate or ask the text questions.

For example, look at the subject in verse 38: Martha.

a. The first fact mentioned answers the question of **what** she did.

Answer: She welcomed Jesus.

The next part of the phrase answers **where** she welcomed Jesus.

Answer: Into her home.

And in verse 39, we learn more about **who** Martha is by observing that "she had a sister called Mary."

b. Now, look at the facts about Mary in verse 39. Following the same example above, what question is the text answering? In other words, the answer will be who, **what**, **when**, **where**, **why**, or **how**. (See the example given on page 112. This notation is not necessary for diagramming.)

1) _____ –was listening

2) _____ –to the Lord's word

3) _____ –seated at His feet.[61]

When you learn to ask the text questions like this, you can create your own worksheet and ask your own questions. In this way, you will not have to rely on another person to ask you the questions for study. Amazing!

For example, look at verse 41. If you were going to ask a question from the text, you might ask the following question:

In Luke 10:41, what specifically does Jesus say about Martha?

1) _____

2) _____ [62]

Do you see it? You can do this on your own!

3. Another thing that stands out when you diagram the text are words of contrast like *but*. Did you notice the distinct contrasts in this passage? What is contrasted in this passage? Hint: Follow the word **but**.

a. _____

b. _____

c. _____ [63]

Slowing down and taking the time to diagram a small portion of Scripture at a time allows you to see things you would never see normally, especially in a casual reading.

INTERPRETATION

Now that you have observed the text, let's work on interpreting what has been said. To do this, you will want to consult a word study and a word study dictionary to help with the Greek words used and identify cross-references in Scripture that use the same word in the same way. Cross-references allow Scripture to interpret Scripture.

1. Look up the passage of Scripture in *The Complete Word Study New Testament*, written by Spiros Zodhiates. (The book is written using the King James Version of the New Testament and is in the order of the books of the Bible.)

Find the book of Luke. Look up Luke 10:38–42.

Here is a sample of what you will find: Note verses 40–42.[64]

1161   art,nn3136   ipf4049   pre4012 an,aj4183   an,nn1248   1161   apta2186

40 But Martha was encumbered about much serving, and came to him,

aina2036 an,nn2962   pin3199/3756/ppro4671   3754 ppro3450 art,nn79   aina2641 ppro3165   pinf1247

and said, Lord, dost*thou*not*care that my sister hath left me to serve

an,aj3440 alma2036 ppro846   3767   2443   asbm4878 ppro3427

alone? bid her therefore that she help me.

1161   art,nn2424   aptp611   aina2036   ppr0846   an,nn3136   an,nn3136

41 And Jesus answered and said unto her, Martha, Martha, thou

pin3309   2532   pinp5182   pre4012   an,ajn4183

art careful and troubled about many things:

1161   nu,ajn1520   pin2076   pr/an,nn5532   1161   an,nn3137   aom1586   art,aj18   an,nn3310

42 But one thing is needful: and Mary hath chosen that good part,

repro3748   3756   fp851   pre575 ppro846

which shall not be taken away from her.

Can you see the letters and numbers above each word?

Next, locate the word you are looking for and record the number so that you can look up its meaning. It's as simple as being able to follow a number. (The numbers used by Zodhiates also correspond with *Strong's Concordance*, which can be very helpful for the purpose of being used together.)

Now that you have the number, you may use *The Word Study* or *The Complete Word Study New Testament Dictionary* by Spiros Zodhiates to look up the meaning of the word and find other cross-references where this word is used in other parts of Scripture.

For example, let's focus on Luke 10:41 in particular. I have diagrammed the section and placed the part of speech and the number of the word above the text.

(an, nn 3136) "**Martha, Martha**

(pin 3309)
you are worried
and
(pinp 5182)   } about so many things
bothered

2. After I diagram, I use the *Word Study* to look up the number of the word for more information. Then I place the number above the word from the text.

3. Next, I look the words up using the corresponding number in *The Word Study Dictionary*.

For example, look at the example below of the word "bothered" using the *Word Study Dictionary*:

4. Next, you will want to find the word and definition and record it.

#5182—The first word is the actual Greek word. The word *turbazo* is the transliterated word in English.

5182. τυρβάζω *turbázō*; fut. *turbásō*, from *túrbē* (n.f.), a crowd, tumult, related to *thórubos* (2351), noise, uproar. To make noise, an uproar, to disturb, stir up. In the NT, figuratively, to disturb in the mind, trouble, make anxious, mid. / pass. (Luke 10:41).

Syn.: *thorubéō* (2350) and *tarássō* (5015), to disturb; *diatarássō* (1298), to agitate greatly; *ektarássō* (1613), to throw into great trouble, agitate; *thlíbō* (2346), to afflict; *enochléō* (1776), to vex; *parenochléō* (3926), to annoy; *skúllō* (4660), to harass, annoy; *anastatóō* (387), to upset, disturb.

Ant.: *hēsucházō* (2270), to be still, quiet; *eirēneúō* (1514), to be at peace; *kopázō* (2869), to relax.

Do you see the definition specifically for Luke 10:41? Zodhiates states, "In the NT (New Testament), figuratively, to disturb in the mind, trouble, make anxious."[65]

Note: You do not need to look up every word. I typically will look up the verbs and any other word that piques my interest. For practice, you may want to follow along and look the words up too. You can compare your notes with mine. For example, when interpreting Luke 10:38–42, I looked at the following words:

a. "Mary, who moreover was **listening** to the Lord's word"

Listening—#191—*akouo*—to hear with attention.[66] (In other words, her mind is engaged.)

b. "Martha was **distracted** with all her preparations"

Distracted—# 4049—*perispaomai*—In the New Testament, it is used figuratively and means to be drawn around in mind or to be distracted, preoccupied with cares or business.[67]

c. "The Lord **answered** and said to her"

Answered—#611—*apekrithen*—to separate, discern, to judge.[68]

d. "Martha, Martha, you are **worried** and **bothered** about so many things"

Worried—#3309—*merimnao*—to be anxious, to take thought.[69]

Bothered—# 5182—*turbazo*—to disturb in the mind.[70]

e. "Mary has **chosen** the good part"

Chosen—#1586—*eklego*—to select, choose for oneself, not necessarily implying the rejection of what is not chosen, but giving favor to the chosen subject, keeping in view a relationship to be established between the one choosing and the object chosen. It involves preference and selection from among many choices.[71]

Remember, it is as easy as following a number. You may also want to look up a different word from the text.

5. As you look at the words and definitions, you will begin to be able to interpret the text more clearly. For example, look at the words above and note the ones that involve the thoughts/mind.

    a. What do you see? _____

    b. Think about the definition for *heart*. Can you see that what Martha thinks controls what Martha does and how she feels? What do you see in regard to her heart?

    c. What did you see specifically about the word "chosen" in Luke 10:42? What does this definition tell you about each of the women and their choice?

    Mary _____

    Martha _____

6. Now, let's look at a cross-reference for help. Notice, Jesus calls Martha by her name and then repeats it. Let's look at some other places in Scripture where Jesus did the same thing and see if there are some parallels from which we can draw. Look up the reference and list the name of the person being called twice, along with what is happening in the verse.

    a. Luke 22:31– _____ , _____ (name)

    What is happening? _____

    b. Acts 9:4– _____ , _____ (name)

    What is happening? _____

    c. Looking at these cross-references, what do you think the Lord is doing by calling Martha by name twice?

7. After you have diagrammed the verses and spent time interpreting the verses using your study tools, it is time to consult a trusted commentary. Oftentimes, we start with a commentary. In this way we are not allowing the Holy Spirit to personally teach and illuminate our minds. We are, in essence, depending on what He has shown another.

Below is an example of the commentator I consulted and the comments I found interesting. This is in no way exhaustive but is here to serve as an example of the commentaries I consulted.

a. I. Howard Marshall, *The New International Greek Testament Commentary: The Gospel of Luke.*

"Mary's posture expresses zeal to learn and it is significant that Jesus encourages a woman to learn from Him, since the Jewish teachers were generally opposed to this."[72]

b. R. H. Stein, *The New American Commentary: Volume 24: Luke.*

"Mary was listening to what He said. 'Listening' is a durative imperfect and emphasizes a continual listening. She was listening to 'what He said' (literally *His word*)."[73]

"What feeds the soul is more important than what feeds the body."[74]

c. T. C. Butler, *Holman New Testament Commentary: Luke.*

"The rabbis had taught people to listen to wise men or teachers but not to talk much with women. Jesus, the wisest of men, welcomed Mary to his audience of learners."[75]

d. John MacArthur, *The MacArthur New Testament Commentary: Luke 6–10.*

"As the story unfolds, it reveals the different reactions of the two sisters (and is common among believers) to the teaching of Jesus: Mary was devoted, but Martha was distracted."[76]

"'**Lord, do You not care**?' To so rebuke the one who is compassionate and gracious and cares for His people is one of the most foolish and graceless statements anyone ever made to Jesus."[77]

"Martha was worried about the bread that feeds the body, while Mary's focus was on the Bread of Life that feeds the soul."[78]

e. Oswald Chambers, *My Utmost for His Highest Journal.*

"The greatest competitor of devotion to Jesus is service for Him."[79]

8. Now, let's put this all together. Look at the word studies, cross-references, and commentaries you have consulted and make an attempt to interpret Luke 10:38–42. Write your thoughts below.

Now, I would like to offer a few biblical interpretations I have seen from the text to serve as an example:

1. Mary's mind was engaged in the words of Jesus (the Word of God). This choice affected what she did and how she felt.

2. Mary's choice was one of preference, not neglect or rejection.

3. Mary had her priorities in order. This affected the order of her mind, will, and emotions.

4. Martha's choice was to neglect the Word with distracting thoughts of service for Him.

5. Martha's choice affected what she did (complained to the Lord and accused Him of not caring) and how she felt (worried and bothered by many things).

6. Martha's preparations for the Lord were her own. Notice the pronoun "her" before the word "preparations." In this case, Martha, in a sense, was master.

7. Martha missed out on a divine appointment that day. How often would she be able to have the Lord Jesus sit in her home and teach her in such a personal and intimate way?

8. Martha's thoughts, like the voice of the enemy, caused her to doubt the character of God ("Lord, do You not care?").

9. The Lord gave Mary, a woman, the opportunity to sit at His feet and learn, unlike the rabbis of that day.

10. Clearly man and God's evaluations are the exact opposite, which is why we need His perspective from the Word to evaluate and think correctly.

11. Martha blamed not only her sister, Mary, but the Lord in this encounter. Sounds a lot like Genesis 3:12–13.

12. The Word of God is the one thing NECESSARY for His disciples!

13. Of all the things that vie for our attention, there is nothing more important to the Lord Jesus than when His disciples listen and obey His Word.

14. We are given the opportunity to choose the good part every day, but we do not always take it.

15. Our evaluation of what is "good" is different from His evaluation of what is "good."

16. The heart of a disciple will want to sit at His feet and listen to His Word.

17. Service for Him will flow out of a heart that has heard from Him and simply responds in obedience.

18. A heart that has not spent time in His Word will eventually respond by complaining about God and others while placing doubt on the character of God.

19. The "many things" can never be a substitute for the "one" thing.

20. "Out of the abundance of the heart, the mouth speaks" (Matt. 12:34, ESV).

21. Mary's posture revealed the attitude of her heart.

22. The issue is never the behavior; the issue is always the attitude of our heart!

The biblical mandate "Be diligent to present yourself approved to God as a workman who does not need to be ashamed, handling accurately the word of truth" (2 Tim. 2:15) clearly begins as we carefully execute the first two steps in the Inductive Method: observation and interpretation.

However, part of handling the Word of God accurately so that we, as His workman, are not ashamed, will be fully realized as we walk in obedience through personal application. As believers, we can deceive ourselves by hearing God's Word and not obeying what He says. We read the Word as if obedience is optional.

Consider the following verse: "But prove yourselves **doers** of the word, and not merely hearers who delude themselves" (James 1:22, emphasis added). Do you see the danger when you "hear" the Word of God but do not "do" what He says by choosing to surrender your will or walk in obedience? What happens?

APPLICATION

If you have observed and interpreted the text adequately, you will find that the application simply falls out of the passage. What has the Lord shown you in regard to application?

Here are some examples of personal applications that might be gleaned after observing and interpreting the text:

1. Do I begin each day sitting at His feet and listening to His Word?

2. Is the Word of God a priority in my daily life?

3. Do I view His Word as the "one" thing necessary?

4. What are the "many things" in my life that are keeping me from the one thing necessary?

5. What/who have I been complaining about lately?

6. If the Lord were to evaluate my life lately, would He use words like *worried* and *bothered*?

7. In what ways have I accused the Lord, either outwardly or inwardly, of not caring?

8. What am I telling Him to do?

9. What is my posture before the Lord? How has the posture of my heart revealed my attitude lately?

10. Are the things that I have been putting into my mind causing me to draw near Him, or are they keeping me from Him?

11. Have I been offering the Lord my service instead of my company?

12. Is your best service for the Lord keeping you from time alone with Him?

13. "Beware of the trap of a performance driven Christian life."[80]

14. "This story is about the priority of the Word of God in our life."[81]

15. "Jesus is saying, 'I want to talk to you about your commitment to Me; rather than your achievement for Me.'"[82]

16. "Attitude comes before activity."[83]

NOTES

CHAPTER 10

TO THE COUNSELOR: "DOES EVERYONE GET WELL?"

"Hear then the parable of the sower."
(Matt. 13:18)

Discipling/counseling another person can be very frustrating, especially when there is little or no fruit. As has been previously stated, you cannot disciple the spiritually dead. And let's face it, there are people who are deceived into thinking they belong to the Lord, and there are those who deceive others into thinking they belong to the Lord. So how can one tell the difference, since we are not even able to judge our own hearts, much less the heart of another? Jesus, in His parable of the sower, can help in our understanding as we attempt to disciple/counsel another person.

Consider the following types of soil presented in Matthew 13:3–9; Mark 4:3–9; and Luke 8:5–8. List the facts from Scripture about each. We will begin by observing the facts from Matthew and add any new information from Mark's and Luke's gospels.

"And He [Jesus] spoke many things to them in parables, saying, 'Behold, the sower went out to sow'" (Matt. 13:3; see also Mark 4:3; Luke 8:5).

OBSERVING THE PARABLE

The seed that fell beside the road:

1. Look at Matthew 13:4 and Mark 4:4 and answer the following questions:

    a. Who came when the seeds were sown and some fell beside the road? _____

    b. What did the birds do with the seeds? _____

2. What information can be added about the seed by looking at Luke 8:5? _____

The seed that fell on the rocky places:

1. Look at Matthew 13:5–6 and Mark 4:5–6 and answer the following questions:

    a. What do you learn about the soil? _____

    b. What happened to the seeds immediately after they were sown? _____

    c. What happened to the seeds when the sun had risen? 1) _____ and

    2) _____

    d. Why did they wither away? _____

2. What information can be added about the soil by looking at Luke 8:6? _____

The seed that fell among the thorns:

1. Look at Matthew 13:7 and answer the following questions:

    a. What came up as the seed was sown? _____

    b. What did the thorns do to the seeds? _____

2. What added information is given in Mark 4:7? _____

3. Now look at Luke 8:7. What do you learn about the relation between the seeds and the thorns?

The seed that fell on the good soil:

1. Look at Matthew 13:8 and answer the following questions:

    a. What happened to the seed that was sown in the good soil? _____

b. What do you learn about the crop?   1) Some _____

2) Some _____

3) Some _____

2. What does Mark 4:8 add about the seeds? _____ and _____

3. Luke 8:8 tells us what Jesus said as He told the parable. What did Jesus call out?

_____

4. What does the seed represent according to Luke 8:11? _____

INTERPRETING THE PARABLE

Jesus said, "Hear then the parable of the sower" (Matt. 13:18).

The seed that fell beside the road:

1. What are the facts regarding this person and the Word of God according to Matthew 13:19?

   a. _____

   b. _____

   c. _____

2. What is the target of the enemy according to Mark 4:15? _____

3. What is the purpose of the Word according to Luke 8:12? In other words, why does the enemy target the Word of God?

   a. _____

   b. _____

Interesting note: In Scripture, typically, the name represents one's character and nature. Did you notice that the enemy is called by three specific names?

4. The names of the enemy:

   a. Matthew 13:19– _____

   b. Mark 4:15– _____

   c. Luke 8:12– _____

If you have access to a word study or online study tools, look up the meaning of each name, which represents the character and nature of the enemy.[84] What do you see?

The seed that fell on the rocky places:

1. What are the facts regarding this person and the Word of God according to Matthew 13:20?

   a. _____

   b. _____

2. What do you learn about this person's heart according to Matthew 13:21?

3. What two things specifically arise according to Matthew 13:21?

   a. _____

   or

   b. _____

4. Did you notice the source of the affliction and persecution? _____

5. Ultimately, what happens to this person? _____

   (Mark 4:16–17 records the same facts.)

6. Do you see any additional facts in Luke 8:13? _____

The seed that fell among the thorns:

1. What are the facts regarding this person and the Word of God according to Matthew 13:22?

2. What is happening to the Word specifically? _____

3. What specifically is choking the Word? (Mark 4:19 and Luke 8:14 add the third fact.)

   a. _____

   b. _____

   c. _____

4. What is the ultimate result of the choking of the word according to Matthew 13:22?

5. Do you see any additional information from Mark 4:19 and Luke 8:14?

The seed that fell on the good soil:

1. What are the facts regarding this person and the Word of God according to Matthew 13:23?

   a.

   b.

2. As a result, what will this person "bear"?

3. How is the heart of this person described in Luke 8:15?

   a.

   b.

4. Is there any additional information provided in Mark 4:20 and Luke 8:15 you would like to add?

ADDITIONAL INFORMATION TO HELP INTERPRET THE PARABLE

At this point, I would like to add some additional insight into the parable of the sower by using word studies and cross-references.[85] This addition is by no means exhaustive.

First, you will easily observe that there are four distinct types of soil, each representing the heart of the one who receives the seed (Matt. 13:19). There is one fact each soil/heart has in common. Notably, each of the four soils "hears the word." The word "hears" is the Greek word *akouo*, which means to hear with understanding and comprehension. This type of hearing involves the volitional (one's ability to choose) aspect of one's will. In other words, to hear the Word of God in this parable would include doing what the Word says.

Each soil/heart is without excuse because each has heard the Word. However, only one soil is labeled by Jesus as "good" because this soil has not only heard with the ear but also understood and comprehended the need to obey what was heard. In essence, only the "good" heart **obeys** the Word of God.

Let's look at each of the soils/hearts and their response to the Word of God as they appear in Scripture.

The seed that fell beside the road:

The seed that fell beside the road represents the heart that hears the Word but does not understand or comprehend it. This is the person who hears the truth but does not obey it. The person represented by the hardened soil is one who chooses not to understand, rather than a person who wants to understand but cannot. Such a person may actually understand Jesus' teaching in a literal sense but refuses to accept its truth.[86]

Paul explains the reason a person does not understand the Word, stating, "And even if our gospel is veiled, it is veiled to those who are perishing, in whose case **the god of this world has blinded the minds of the unbelieving**, that they might not see the light of the gospel of the glory of Christ, who is the image of God" (2 Cor. 4:3–4, emphasis added).

Likewise, Scripture states, "But a natural man does not accept the things of the Spirit of God; for they are foolishness to him, and **he cannot understand** them, because they are spiritually appraised" (1 Cor. 2:14; emphasis added).

Furthermore, Luke 8:5 adds insight into the text by stating that the seed was "trampled under foot." The word "trampled" is the word *katapateo*, which means "to treat with utmost contempt and indignity." In essence, this is the heart that does not want to hear the Word of God. This heart is not seeking truth. It has no intention of doing what the Word of God commands. This is a hard heart, and its end is destruction.

MacArthur describes this heart:

> This is the heart that knows no repentance, no sorrow over sin, no guilt, and no concern for the things of God. It allows itself to be trampled by an endless procession of evil thoughts, cherished sins, and ungodly activities. It is careless, callous, and indifferent—never broken up or softened by conviction or sorrow for wrongdoing. This is the heart of the fool described in Proverbs. He hates knowledge. He resists instruction. He despises wisdom.[87]

Moreover, the enemy, specifically referred to by Matthew as the "evil one" (Matt. 13:19), takes advantage of this type of heart and sees this as an opportunity to come and snatch the seed away. The verb "comes" is in the middle voice, meaning the subject (the evil one) initiates and participates in the action. It is also in the present tense, meaning this is a continuous action. The term "snatches away" is the Greek word *harpazio*, which means "to seize upon with force." Peter vividly describes the enemy's manner and activity, warning, "Be of sober spirit, be on the alert. Your adversary, the devil, prowls about like a roaring lion, seeking someone to devour" (1 Pet. 5:8).

Interestingly, each of the Synoptic Gospel writers employs a different yet specific name to paint a vivid picture of the enemy's character and intent. Matthew's choice of the term "evil one," or *ho poneros*, literally means "wicked and malicious." This name describes one whose desire is to entice another into the evil as a trap or vice. Mark's gospel uses the name Satan, which means "adversary, or one who tempts believers and unbelievers." Luke uses the term "devil," which is the Greek word *diabolos*, meaning "to accuse/ slander; one who divides people."

Notice the enemy's target is always the Word of God. Luke gives us insight as to why: "so that they may not believe and be saved" (Luke 8:12). This statement is in keeping with what Paul says in Romans 10:17: "Faith comes from hearing, and hearing by the word of Christ." The enemy knows that the Spirit of God uses the Word of God for faith and salvation. Therefore, should we use anything other than God's Word for matters of faith and salvation? John MacArthur states, "There is no such thing as evangelism apart from God's Word."[88]

The message to the one sowing the seed is clear. There will be opposition. The enemy will act wickedly and maliciously in an effort to tempt, accuse, and slander God's Word. He will set his mark on the Word of God as well as those who sow it. But take heart. God says, "I am watching over My word to perform it" (Jer. 1:12). And Isaiah reminds us that when He sends forth His Word, it will accomplish what He desires (Isa. 55:11).

This type of heart condition is easy to identify and more than likely will not be seeking discipleship or counsel. However, the next two soils listed in Scripture are a little more difficult to assess and identify. Outwardly, they will profess Christ, but when they encounter difficulties or temptations because of the Word of God, they will reveal their true inward state, and it will become more evident that they do not possess Christ.

Let's look at the next two soils more closely since you will inevitably encounter many of these hearts as you continue to disciple/counsel others.

The seed that fell upon the rocky places:

The seed that fell upon the rocky places represents the heart of the one who, by all appearances, loves the Word and receives it immediately with great joy. This heart is also described as having "no **firm** root in himself" and "is only temporary" (Matt. 13:21, emphasis added).

What does it mean when a heart has no firm root? In this passage, the word "root" is used figuratively and means "to be established in faith or doctrine." Basically, the heart of this individual is not established in biblical doctrine. Therefore, their faith is only temporary and will last as long as things go smoothly in their life. We see this today in much of "Christian" television where the listener is promised "health, wealth, and prosperity"—as long as you first send in your "seed money," of course. The Bible would describe this teaching as false. This mentality is problematic because Jesus warns the believer there will be times of trouble and persecution. In fact, He clearly states, "Remember the word I said to you, 'A slave is not greater than his master.' If they persecuted Me, they will also persecute you" (John 15:20). Paul also warned Timothy, stating, "All who desire to live godly in Christ Jesus will be persecuted" (2 Tim. 3:12).

MacArthur comments on this type of heart today:

The superficial response is epidemic in twenty-first-century Christianity. Why? Because the gospel is usually presented with the promise of joy, warmth, fellowship, and a good feeling, but without the hard demand to take up one's cross and follow Christ. "Converts" are not confronted with the real issues of sin and repentance. Instead, they are encouraged to jump on the Jesus bandwagon for the good things they are promised. Yet underneath the shallow layer of apparently fertile topsoil is an unyielding rock bed of rebellion and resistance to the things of God. There is no true repentance, no brokenness, and no contrition.[89]

In the parable, this heart is truly revealed when affliction and persecution appear. The word "affliction" (Matt. 13:21) has the meaning of being squeezed under pressure. This can prove to be detrimental when the person squeezed under pressure has no firm root from within. When pressed, what is inside will come out. The person with this type of heart, when under affliction or suffering persecution, will inevitably fall away. The term "falls away" in this verse is the Greek word *skandalizo*, from which the English words *scandal* or *scandalous* is derived. Notably, the source of the affliction and persecution is the Word of God!

Bible scholar Leon Morris expounds on the term "falls away":

> Most translations say that he "falls away" . . . but there is something more than falling. He *takes offense*. That is to say, he comes to regard adherence to Christ as something of a trap; if it means persecution he wants nothing to do with it. He is repelled. The time of trial means the end of this person's adherence to Christ.[90]

Sadly, there are many today who joyfully profess Christ and yet abandon Him when the circumstances of life squeeze them into a corner. The health, wealth, and prosperity gospel will not hold firm when there is affliction and persecution. When squeezed, this heart must choose to either obey the Word of God or desert. MacArthur warns, "Be on guard against conversions that are all smiles and cheers with no sense of repentance or humility. That is the mark of a superficial heart."[91]

Afflictions and persecution are refining agents that provide a sort of litmus test for the superficial heart. For the unbeliever, they will serve to expose the rebellion and sin within. Persecution and affliction have a way of removing the fakes. However, for the believer, they will serve to strengthen and refine the heart. They are used by God to help remove the dross and impurities in our hearts. They are the agents used by God whereby we become more and more conformed to the image of Christ (Rom. 8:28–29).

The seed that fell among the thorns:

The third scenario Jesus describes in the parable of the sower is the seed that fell among the thorns. This is the heart that has no room for God's Word because it is so crowded with a love for the world and the things of the world. This heart represents the double-minded man whom James describes as being "unstable in all his ways" (James 1:8). This person may be described today as having "one foot in the church and one foot in the world."

This man is described in Matthew 13:22 as one who "hears the word" but allows specific things to "choke the word"—namely, the "worry of the world," "the deceitfulness of riches," and the desires or "pleasures of this life" (Luke 8:14). Luke's gospel points out the fact that this person hears the Word, "**as they go on their way**" (Luke 8:14: emphasis added). The phrase "as they go on their way" is quite telling. Scripture warns, "There is a way which seems right to a man, but its end is the way of death" (Prov. 14:12). A person cannot choose to go his or her own way and follow the way of the Lord. Jesus clearly taught the cost of being His disciple when He said, "If anyone wishes to come after Me, let him deny himself, and take up his cross daily, and follow Me" (Luke 9:23). So what does it look like when a man or a woman chooses to "go on their way"? Scripture gives us three characteristics. Let's examine each of these characteristics individually.

First, the "worries" of the world is the Greek word *merimna*, which means "anxiety or care that brings disruption to the personality and mind." Is this not what is happening in America today? More and more Americans are being treated with behavioral medications because of an increase in anxiety and depression. Unfortunately, this seems to be a growing trend, even in the church. Will the church of Jesus Christ allow the Word of God to become "choked" out by the thorns of anxiety and depression?

Second, Jesus identifies the "deceitfulness of riches" as a means whereby the Word of God can become "choked." Jesus, in one of the most incredible sermons ever preached, made a very clear distinction, stating, "No one can serve two masters; for either he will hate the one and love the other, or he will hold to one and despise the other. You cannot serve God and mammon" (Matt. 6:24). Likewise, Paul warned Timothy about the deceitfulness of riches, stating, "But those who want to get rich fall into temptation and a snare and many foolish and harmful desires which plunge men into ruin and destruction. For the love of money is a root of all sorts of evil, and some by longing for it have wandered away from the faith, and pierced themselves with many a pang" (1 Tim. 6:9–10). John also addresses this heart, stating, "If anyone loves the world, the love of the Father is not in him" (1 John 2:15). There is no doubt from God's Word that the deceitfulness of riches is a thorn that will "choke" the Word of God.

Third, Mark's gospel delineates the "desires for other things [that] enter in" (Mark 4:19), while Luke describes the third characteristic as the "pleasures of this life" (Luke 8:14). Both Mark and Luke are saying the same thing. The term "desires" is the Greek word *epithumia*, which means "lustful/inordinate desires; carnal appetites. All these desires are fixed on sensual objects as pleasures, profits, and honors."[92] The word "pleasures" is the Greek word *hedone*, which means "sensual pleasure, which in the NT is used only of physical pleasure."[93] The phrase "enter in" is used metaphorically and means "to arise, to spring up in the mind." It is also noteworthy that the phrase "enter in" is in the passive voice, meaning that the subject is acted upon. In other words, when the Word of God is "choked" by the thorn of the pleasures/desires of this life, the subject no longer chooses; rather, he or she is acted upon by the pleasures/desires of this life. This is a frightening thought!

Now, let's examine what it means when the Word of God is "choked." The term "choked" literally means "to suffocate/strangle"; used figuratively, it means "to overpower." And even more significant than the meaning of the word is that the tense, mood, and voice of the verb are in the present indicative middle. The present tense denotes continuous action, indicative mood implies factual, and middle voice indicates that the subject is initiating and participating in the action. In essence, this is the heart that hears, understands, and comprehends the Word of God. However, because this heart is divided, and one cannot serve two masters, this heart chooses to continuously initiate and participate in the choking of God's Word. The subject chooses to allow the worries of this world, the deceit of riches, and the pleasures/desires of this life to suffocate or strangle the Word of God. The devastating result of these willful choices is a heart that becomes "unfruitful" (Matt. 13:22), and they can "bring no fruit to maturity" (Luke 8:14).

MacArthur refers to this heart as a "weedy heart." He states, "Weedy hearts may be willing to accept Jesus as Savior, but not if it means letting go of the world. That is not salvation."[94]

The seed that fell on the good soil:

And last, we will examine the seed that fell on the good soil. But first, we must explore the meaning of the word "good," since it is a commonly used word today. The word used in this parable is the Greek word *kalos*, which means "constitutionally good; good as to quality and character." Qualifying the definition, Zodhiates explains, "A person can be made *kalos*, good, what God is, through faith in Jesus Christ, but only insofar as he is a partaker of God's nature (2 Pet. 1:4)."[95] Luke actually describes the characteristics of the heart of this person by using the terms "honest and good" together (Luke 8:15). In this text, the term "honest" is actually a characteristic of the word *kalos*. And the word "good" is the Greek word *agathos*, which is used in a moral sense to mean "upright and virtuous." In actuality, this soil depicts a heart of one who is honest, upright, and virtuous.

Jesus Himself gives even more significance to the meaning of the word "good" when He refers to God alone as being good (Mark 10:18; Luke 18:19). Therefore, I can consider a heart "good" if it is occupied by a "good" God. Only a heart with God in it can be honest, upright, and virtuous.

Now that we have established the definition of a "good" heart, we need to look at the response of this heart to God's Word. According to Matthew's gospel, the good heart both "hears" and "understands" the Word (Matt. 13:23). In other words, this is the heart that hears, comprehends, and obeys God's Word. In regard to God's Word, in the place of the word "understands," used in Matthew, the expression Mark uses is the word "accept" (Mark 4:20).

The word "accept" literally means "to embrace with assent and obedience." In other words, this heart hears the Word of God and surrenders his will to God's will by obeying what God says.

Matthew, Mark, and Luke each record that the good soil that hears and obeys God's Word will ultimately result in bearing fruit. MacArthur, commenting on the good soil, states, "Fruit-bearing is the whole point of agriculture. It is also the ultimate test of salvation."[96] Citing further proof, MacArthur quotes from Matthew 7:17–20, where Jesus states, "Every good tree bears good fruit; but the bad tree bears bad fruit. A good tree cannot produce bad fruit, nor can a bad tree produce good fruit. Every tree that does not bear good fruit is cut down and thrown into the fire. So then, you will know them by their fruits." MacArthur concludes, stating, "Fruit, not foliage, is the mark of true salvation."[97]

So what would the fruit of the Spirit look like in the life of a believer? According to Paul, the fruit produced by God's Spirit would include specific characteristics: "love, joy, peace, patience, kindness, goodness, faithfulness, gentleness, self-control" (Gal. 5:22–23). The believer who surrenders his will to God's Word in obedience will bear the fruit of God's Spirit.

Similarly, consider Paul's prayer on behalf of the church in Colossae. Specifically, Paul has one request: that they would be "filled with the knowledge of His will in all spiritual wisdom and understanding" (Col. 1:9). What does it mean to be "filled with the knowledge of His will"? We become filled with the knowledge of His will when we surrender our will in obedience to His will—namely, His Word. Now consider the effects or results of this prayer. Paul continues: "So that you may walk in a manner worthy of the Lord, to please Him in all respects, **bearing fruit in every good work** and increasing in the knowledge of God; strengthened with all power, according to His glorious might, for the attaining of all steadfastness and patience; joyously giving thanks to the Father" (Col. 1:10–12, emphasis added).

Now consider this. Which comes first? The fruit bearing or being filled with the knowledge of His will? Furthermore, consider that Matthew's and Mark's gospels specify the extent of the fruit bearing to include thirty, sixty, and a hundredfold (Matt. 13:23; Mark 4:20). Noting the difference in productivity, MacArthur states, "Not every Christian will always bear as much fruit as he or she ought to or could. Christians are sometimes disobedient, and of course they still sin."[98]

Interestingly, the late theologian Arthur Pink made a correlation between the levels of fruit productivity with the levels of spiritual maturity listed in 1 John 2:12–14. For example, a spiritual baby would produce thirtyfold, a young man would produce sixtyfold, and the spiritual father would produce a hundredfold.[99] One thing is certain—a person who is willing to surrender his will and obey God's Word will bear fruit. However, one must consider that the level or degree of productivity may have to do with the willing submission and obedience on the part of the believer.

We must also consider that Luke includes the fact that those who bear fruit will do so with perseverance (Luke 8:15). Although there is only one word in the English language for the word "perseverance," there are two words used in the Greek language, which help differentiate the object of the perseverance.

For example, *makrothumia* is used specifically in regard to people, whereas *hupomone* is the word chosen when facing difficult circumstances and includes suffering in faith and duty. The specific word used in Luke 8:15 is *hupomone*, which indicates suffering in and through difficult circumstances. Only the Spirit of God in an individual can bear this type of fruit (Gal. 5:22–23).

As for the one who sows the seed, the late pastor and theologian Charles Spurgeon stated:

> The preacher of the gospel is like the sower. He does not make his seed; it is given him by his divine Master. No man could create the smallest grain that ever grew upon the earth, much less the celestial seed of eternal life! The minister goes to his Master in secret, and asks him to teach him his gospel, and thus he fills his basket with the good seed of the kingdom. He then goes forth in his Master's name and scatters precious truth. If he knew where the best soil was to be found, perhaps he might limit himself to that which had been prepared by the plough of conviction; but not knowing men's hearts, it is his business to preach the gospel to every creature—to throw a handful on the hardened heart, and another on the mind which is overgrown with the cares and pleasures of the world. He has to leave the seed in the care of the Lord who gave it to him, for he is not responsible for the harvest, he is only accountable for the care and industry with which he does his work. If no single ear should ever make glad the reaper, the sower will be rewarded by his Master if he had planted the right seed with careful hand.[100]

As we consider the fourth soil, we are reminded of what the Lord God promised long ago through the prophet Ezekiel: "I will give you a new heart and put a new spirit within you; I will remove the heart of stone from your flesh and give you a heart of flesh. And I will put My Spirit within you and cause you to walk in My statutes, and you will be careful to observe My ordinances" (Ezek. 36:26–27).

Do you see it? When we accept Jesus Christ as our Lord and Savior, He gives us a new heart and sends His Spirit to live in us. God's Spirit then becomes the **cause** of our ability to obey God. Apart from God in us, we will not obey Him. Our hearts will not and cannot be good apart from the "good" God within. Truly, we are in desperate need of Him!

A FINAL SUMMATION OF THE PARABLE OF THE SOWER

In conclusion, as you look at the four soils and evaluate each in light of the definition of the word *faith*, we see a glaring difference.

For example, FAITH is . . .

1. a firm conviction of God's Word (God's Spirit using God's Word);

2. a personal surrender of the will to God's Word;

3. obedience to God's Word.

Clearly the first three soils represent the person who does not have a faith that saves. Although they may have made a mental assent to God's Word for a time, their "faith" is merely a head knowledge. They lack a true heart knowledge because they fail to surrender their will and obey God's Word despite the afflictions, persecutions, and temptations that will inevitably come their way. Only the fourth soil qualifies as a biblical saving faith. Only the fourth soil is truly "good." *Which soil are you? Ask the Spirit of truth to lead you to the truth.*

To the biblical counselor/discipler, let this parable serve as a reminder that not everyone you counsel will be "good" soil. Let it also serve as an encouragement as you continue to do your part, which is to sow the seed of God's Word and leave the results to Him!

NOTES

CHAPTER 11

"Heal me, O LORD, and I will be healed; Save me and I will be saved,

For Thou art my praise."

(Jer. 17:14)

As you may have noticed, in the last chapter not everyone gets well. This chapter, however, is dedicated to those whom the Lord has led to surrender their wills to His will and obey His Word with reckless abandon. The names of the people in the vignettes have been changed to protect their identities. However, the stories you will read are authentic testimonies of hearts that have been transformed by the power of God's Spirit and His Word.

The purpose of this workbook is to provide a biblical model of discipleship that will lead others to spiritual maturity. The purpose of this chapter is to provide examples of real-life encounters, which will help to both encourage and instruct you as you continue in the process of discipleship.

HANNAH'S STORY

Hannah is a sixty-five-year-old grandmother of two who presented initially with weight issues. Under the surface, however, the problems were much deeper. Upon examining 1 John 2:12–14, Hannah discovered that she was spiritually weak, being overcome by the enemy in many areas, especially her thought life, and despite many years of Bible study, the Word of God did not abide within her in a consistent life-changing way. In short, Hannah discovered that despite being raised in church and being saved at the tender age of eleven, she was still a spiritual baby.

Upon examining Jeremiah 1:10, Hannah began to ask the Holy Spirit what exactly needed to be plucked up from her life. She said,

> For years I had lived with anger, resentment, and anxiety. I could not overcome the anger and resentment that consumed me. To comfort myself or find some measure of relief, I would eat. Gluttony ruled my

life. I had outbursts. My mind was paralyzed with fear and confusion. These sins were eating me alive. At times, I seemed to be consumed by what I will describe as "murderous anger." I hated everyone and everything. I hated myself and was desperate for change. I went to the Lord time after time and attended Bible study after Bible study, trying to rid myself of my sin. I would get another "religious" self-help book with three steps to peace and happiness. I would follow the steps and for a few days experience some success, but sadly, I would find myself in the same pit, only it was a little deeper and a whole lot darker.

Upon examining Genesis 3 with specific reference to the heart, the Holy Spirit began to uncover emotions Hannah had tried to conceal for years. For example, when evaluating the emotion of anger, Hannah prayed and asked the Lord what she was covering, hiding, or blaming on others in regard to this emotion. The Spirit of truth began to take her back to her childhood, which invoked memories of her mother. While talking about what a wonderful mother she had, Hannah stated, "One time, when I was five or six years old, my mother locked me in a dark smokehouse for hours." When asked why she was locked in a dark smokehouse, Hannah defended her mother by explaining what a "bad little girl" she had been. When asked what she had done, she would recall incidents where she had not obeyed by picking up her toys or cleaning her room when told. Hannah recalls, "What I can remember vividly is the times Momma disciplined me by telling me that she was going to leave and never come home again. I lived with that fear of her leaving me all through my childhood."

When I stated, "So, your mother abused you when you were a little girl?" Hannah immediately responded by defending her mother and stating that she had been a good mother. This went on for several minutes. When asked if she had disciplined her own son in that manner, she stated, "Oh, NO!" When asked why not, she broke down into tears and said, "Because that would have scared him to death!" Just as the Holy Spirit so often will do when He is plucking up, sometimes He takes the disciple back to the place where the fear initially surfaced.

Hannah had convinced herself that her mother's actions were justified because of her misbehavior. She had believed the lie that she was the problem and had hidden the abuse all her life to protect her mother's reputation. In essence, she was listening to the wrong voice—the voice that does not align with Scripture.

Similarly, when the emotions of anger and resentment surfaced, the Holy Spirit revealed to her a memory that had been concealed for years, a time in her early teens when a much older brother-in-law had touched her inappropriately. When Hannah told her mother, she was met with accusations that somehow she had probably enticed him.

She was informed that the matter was never to be spoken of again. After tracing her emotions past the anger and resentment, and looking back at the sin that had been hidden, she was able to identify the voice who told her that this was a result of what she deserved.

Once again, the voice of the enemy had begun to influence her mind, which affected her actions and emotional state.

In looking back over this time, Hannah recalls, "The realization that I had been listening to the enemy was a gradual one. As I took steps of obedience, I could see more and more that I had been obeying the voice of the enemy."

During this time, Hannah was given an assignment to make a list on one side of a legal pad of the thoughts that seemed to control her mind no matter how ugly, sinful, or shameful. On the other side of the paper, she was asked to align those thoughts with Scripture. If she could not align them with Scripture, she was to search the Word of God for the truth. For example, one of the thoughts she had written down was "I should have never been born." She said her mother had repeatedly told her this because of the fact that she was an "accident," born when her mother was in her forties. Realizing this statement did not align with the Word, Psalm 139:13-14 came to mind: "For Thou didst form my inward parts; Thou didst weave me in my mother's womb. I will give thanks to Thee, for I am fearfully and wonderfully made; wonderful are Thy works, and my soul knows it very well." When asked if her "soul knew it very well," she wept.

Similarly, the thought that her mother would leave her—a thought that had paralyzed her with fear for years—was replaced. Hannah observed, "I learned to trust the ONE who will never leave or forsake me" (see Heb. 13:5). Choosing to listen to the correct voice is paramount in having a sound mind. Hannah began to choose to listen to God's Word and, in so doing, became able to identify the voice of the enemy. Hannah reports, "I still listen to the wrong voice at times. But now, I can identify the voice, and I am quick to refuse to listen. I make the choice to align those voices of fear and worry with the Word of God. As I allow my thoughts to be transformed by the Word, the torment of fear leaves."

Throughout the months of discipleship, the Holy Spirit was faithful to lead her to the truth, not only in regard to the sin others had committed against her, but also of the sinful choices she had willfully chosen (John 16:13). For example, the Holy Spirit revealed a deep-seated bitterness that had taken root from a failed marriage. Even after years of asking the Lord to forgive her for the divorce, Hannah was still plagued with hurt, unforgiveness, and shame. When asked if she had made things right with the former husband, she stated, "No." After asking the Holy Spirit if she needed to ask for his forgiveness, she was taken to Matthew 5:23-24. After realizing her need to ask for his forgiveness for her part in the failed marriage and divorce, Hannah contacted the former husband and asked for forgiveness for the sin she had committed against him. Instantly, she sensed relief from the hurt, unforgiveness, and shame. To date, Hannah has not experienced these emotions again, despite many years of carrying this heavy baggage.

The freedom she has experienced has been life-changing. So often one is quick to ask the Lord for forgiveness yet never ask forgiveness from the one who was wronged. One cannot help but wonder, What would the church be like if this happened on a regular basis? Is this not what Jesus meant when He declared that the second greatest command is to "love your neighbor as yourself" (Matt. 22:39)? How can one say they love God if they can sin against their neighbor and never ask for her or his forgiveness if needful?

Throughout the discipleship process, Hannah learned to surrender her will and obey the Word of God. As a result, she has found great peace and freedom. By allowing the Lord to pluck up and destroy the things in her past, Hannah is experiencing the Lord's peace, joy, and great love as He plants, builds, and restores "the years that the . . . locust has eaten" (Joel 2:25). As a result of her testimony, many women are learning to find liberty in Christ as well.

PHOEBE'S STORY

After meeting Phoebe, one would hardly believe that behind her big smile and charismatic personality was a woman who was hurting deeply. As a child, Phoebe was told she had been "accidentally" conceived, after which her birth mother was counseled by her maternal grandmother to abort. She was then given up for adoption to parents who would eventually divorce. Later in life, she again experienced rejection from her first husband. However, when she recalls these devastating childhood and adult memories, she simply smiles and says, "It is really okay; I am all right." The walls of self-protection were fortified and lofty. They were so strong, even Phoebe did not realize the level of self-deception she had learned to live with her entire life—that is, until she entered into His Word for herself on a deeper level by learning how to handle God's Word correctly.

Outwardly, Phoebe was the picture of a woman who seemed to have it all together. But she admitted she was medicating daily with several anti-anxiety meds and antidepressants her doctor had prescribed. She states, "I had a lot of anxious thoughts and fears I felt rejection, not only by those closest to me but also by God. I had a difficult time believing what the Bible told me about God's love and acceptance. I believed it was true for others, but not for me."

After clearing her calendar and busy schedule, the Lord had impressed upon Phoebe that He was preparing her for something "big and time-consuming." Little did she realize that He was about to set her free from a lifetime of rejection filled with painful memories. Phoebe admits to having participated in numerous Bible studies in the thirty-eight years since she accepted Christ as her Lord and Savior; however, she states, "While those studies did help me strive to be a better Christian, there was no real power or personal trans formation. I remember thinking, *I must be doing something wrong* or *Maybe I did not have enough faith.* At times, it was frustrating, and I felt like there must be more."

Initially, Phoebe was drawn to yet another Bible study because of a deep hunger and desire to live the abundant life that Christ offered, coupled with an urging within her spirit to set apart this specific time in her life. After hearing the Word that first day, Phoebe stayed after class to speak with me and ask for help.

After examining 1 John 2:12–14, Phoebe could clearly see she was spiritually immature. She recalls, "The Lord showed me that I was a child. I was being tossed about and led by my emotions and by the emotions of those around me. I had no victory over the enemy, which was having a negative effect on my marriage and family. It caused me to be more controlling in my relationship with my husband, which caused conflict."

Phoebe admits that she had built up walls so that no one could see or know the "real" Phoebe. Her fear was that if someone got to know her, they would reject her, so Phoebe rejected people first. Despite hearing the Word every week and attempting to read His Word on a regular basis, Phoebe states, "His Word did not abide in me." In Jeremiah 1:10, Phoebe was able to see that the Lord uses His Word as an instrument to surgically remove all the infected areas of her heart. She learned that the areas she had hidden all her life would now be open to exposure and healing if she would allow it. She states, "The Lord showed me He was not going to build on my emotional and spiritual junk."

A pivotal time for Phoebe occurred when she learned the definitions for *faith* and the *heart*. To Phoebe, faith had been an intellectual assent. She did not realize the necessity of the personal surrender of her will coupled with obedience to His Word. Similarly, as Phoebe began to understand that her heart comprises her mind, will, and emotions, and that keeping them in proper sequence is a necessity, she began to see how emotionally driven she really had become. She recalls, "I learned that I had to take God at His Word. I had to choose to believe His Word despite how I felt. I had to surrender my will for His and walk in obedience."

These truths became evident to Phoebe through the ministry of reconciliation (2 Cor. 5:18). Phoebe observes, "Part of pulling up the lies of rejection was going to those who had rejected me, both believers and nonbelievers, and asking for their forgiveness for the bitterness and resentment I had held in my heart toward them." After going to everyone the Holy Spirit brought to mind, Phoebe discovered the biggest offense she had held was against the Lord. This offense, by far, was the heaviest and was heartbreaking. She wept for hours when the Lord revealed this truth. For Phoebe, reconciliation with others is precious; however, reconciliation with the Lord is priceless.

Another crucial time in the discipleship process for Phoebe came while examining Genesis 3. She states, "I learned that the enemy is always speaking and trying to cast doubt on God's Word and His character. He is constantly attacking our thoughts, and the battle is in our minds. The enemy will always win the battle if we come to fight without our weapon, God's Word." Additionally, Phoebe learned that the enemy does not fight fair. She states, "The enemy speaks when we are most vulnerable. He comes when we are tired, alone, hungry, and physically sick."

When Phoebe was asked, "When did you realize you were listening to the wrong voice?" she replied, "Immediately upon going to God's Word as the source of truth and guidance. I learned that the enemy and my fleshly emotions are in agreement and that they war against God's truth." Phoebe has learned that the voices in her head must be in alignment with the truth of God's Word, no matter how she feels.

When the root issue of rejection was first revealed, Phoebe was sent home with a list of Scriptures and statements displaying God's genuine character and attributes on the right side of the page, while the left side listed lying descriptions oftentimes attributed to Him.

For example, on the left side of the page, the words *distant* and *disinterested* were used to describe God. Similarly, on the right side of the page were the words *intimate* and *involved*, along with the corresponding passage of Psalm 139:1–18.

Phoebe was instructed to prayerfully ask the Holy Spirit what she had truly believed about the Lord God. As she began the process, the Holy Spirit revealed to her that for years Phoebe had believed the lies from the enemy in regard to her heavenly Father. As the Holy Spirit began to reveal the truth, Phoebe confessed the lie from the enemy and asked the Lord for forgiveness for having believed the lie rather than the truth of His Word. After confessing her sin of unbelief, Phoebe was instructed to choose between the lie on the left side of the page and the truth on the right side of the page. She allowed the Holy Spirit to reveal to her the truth from the Scripture passage assigned to each attribute. This assignment occurred over a period of several hours in one night.

In an attempt to describe that night in particular, Phoebe states,

> The Lord revealed to me, through intense discipling, that both my birth family and my adoptive family rejected God and, as a result, passed down the generational sin of unbelief and rebellion. He also revealed that in His sovereignty, He had allowed all this in my life. As a result, I would be able to choose to bow to Him and accept that His ways are not my ways and that He is God and I am not. The Lord showed me from His Word that He had allowed me to be sifted due to sin and rebellion from my own pride. Most importantly, He allowed this because of my unbelief. He wanted me to see that He is good and loving, despite how I may "feel," and that He is enough. He revealed to me that I sought comfort in people and various medications yet never really allowed anyone to get too close to me for fear of being rejected again. God, in His mercy, showed me that I had become my own defender and that taking this position was sin. The Holy Spirit showed me that the Lord had been holding me in His arms my entire life and that He had me the whole time (Isa. 43:2–4a). He revealed to me that He had never rejected or forsaken me and that not only had He always been there, but He would always be (Heb. 13:5). He also revealed to me that He alone was my strong tower (Prov. 18:10) and my deliverer (Ps. 40:17).
>
> After asking the Lord for forgiveness for all the lies I had believed for years, I slept the sweetest sleep I have ever experienced. The next morning, He graciously revealed the purpose for my suffering. The following thoughts came to mind: "Your early life represents a generation and what has happened to them (my physical family). They do not love Me or My ways because they had no covering, no spiritual heritage. Therefore, the generational sin and rebellion have been passed down to them. They are the ones younger than you. You must tell them (as I bring them to you) what I have shown you so that they can be saved and live" (2 Cor. 1:3–4). The Lord also showed me that despite my prior unbelief, I could

trust Him to increase my faith (Mark 9:23–24), and that faith creates complete dependence upon the Lord and not independence.

LYNNE'S STORY

Lynne's story can be described as a "divine appointment." Lynne arrived at my house one evening to drop off a baby gift. When invited inside the house, Lynne began with small talk, which soon took on a more serious nature. Lynne expressed a desire to know how to study the Word of God. She confessed that when she read the Bible, she had a difficult time understanding it. One must realize that conversations like this are not accidental; rather, they are providential. I immediately invited Lynne to enter into one-on-one discipleship training on how to study the Bible using the Inductive Method. Lynne was thrilled and agreed immediately.

While searching for a time and date to meet, I mentioned a prior commitment involving discipleship counseling. Immediately, Lynne's countenance changed, and she began to weep. She stated, "I think I need to do that first. I need to tell you something that I have never told anyone, except my husband and a Christian counselor at church." With tears streaming down her face, she said in a trembling voice, "My grandfather molested me when I was a little girl." Over the next several months, Lynne began a process of healing and forgiveness that would transform her heart, her home, and her newfound ministry in Christ.

Beginning with the diagnostic tool found in 1 John 2:12–14, Lynne was not surprised to discover that she was a spiritual baby. The past abuse, coupled with almost forty years of unforgiveness, bitterness, and great pain, had left her spiritually weak, overcome by the enemy, and in desperate need of the healing Word of God. The toll of the abuse and subsequent unforgiveness had manifested not only in spiritual ways but also in physical ways. Lynne was unable to sleep at night. She recalls, "Oftentimes, I do not get more than two to three hours of sleep." Lynne was in desperate need of the Great Physician who would use the Word of God for her treatment.

While assessing the diagnostic process from 1 John 2:12–14, Lynne stated, "The Holy Spirit showed me that I was still like that little child who had been abused. I was weak. The Word of God did not abide in me, so it was easy for Satan to overcome me. I was ashamed and embarrassed of my past. I lived in the fear that people would find out about my past."

The healing process for Lynne began with Jeremiah 1:10, where she discovered that the Lord wanted to uproot and destroy the fear, anger, and unforgiveness that had been devastating her. The Lord used Jeremiah 1:10, coupled with Genesis 3, as a tool to help Lynne uncover the damaging effects and costliness of her sin. For example, during one of the discipleship sessions, after prayer the Holy Spirit reminded Lynne of a time when she was at home after a chemotherapy treatment for breast cancer when she became very angry with her mother. She states, "I became increasingly angry with my mother, knowing that she was there cooking, doing laundry, and helping with my three boys. The voice of the enemy (although I did not recognize it then) said, 'Where was she back then, when you really needed her?'"

Lynne realized her anger stemmed from blaming her mother for not shielding her from such horrific abuse. She felt justified in her anger, since her mother, who had also been a victim of this man's abuse, should have known better and provided protection. Lynne stated, "I kept thinking, 'Why would she leave me with him after what he had done to her?'" Lynne was not the only victim of her grandfather's sin. In fact, Lynne recalls, "I personally did not know he had abused others until several years after his death. My mom and others knew about their own abuse, and that he had abused my cousin. My cousin had the courage to come forward, but it was swept under the rug."

Additionally, Lynne struggled with anger and resentment toward her father for divorcing her mother. The divorce had devastated their family and was one of the reasons her mother had to keep working to support the family. Lynne observes, "My mom always worked. After my parents divorced, my mom worked her regular job at the insurance company, worked on the weekends at the bowling alley snack bar, and worked evenings at McDonalds to keep our family off welfare." One of Lynne's jobs was to keep the house clean and make sure her mother heard her alarm when napping before heading off to her second and third jobs. Lynne says, "Technically, I was left with my grandfather more while my parents were still married. My dad frequently stopped at bars after work, so my mom really could not rely on his help."

One of the most painful memories the Lord brought to the surface was her grandfather's funeral. She described the scene at the Baptist church they had regularly attended, how she had watched as the pastor hailed her grandfather as a respected deacon and servant of the church. With tears streaming from her eyes, she recalled, "I sat there as the pastor spoke and thought, *If you only knew the man I knew*." Now that her grandfather had died, Lynne had begun to focus her hurt and anger on her mother. This, in turn, would leave her feeling very guilty because she loved her mother.

In retrospect, after observing Jeremiah 1:10, Lynne states, "I realized before I could grow as a child of God and be His disciple, He had to show me all the ways I was bound up. God had to open my eyes to the truth so I could understand who He really is." As Lynne began to see God from His Word, she started to see herself and her sin. She states,

> The Lord had to expose all the lies that were truth in my mind. He had to break down my pride by calling it sin. He showed me how to pray, listen, obey, and wait for His Word. Each time I would allow the Holy Spirit to plow (by praying, listening, obeying, and waiting), He would tear down a wall of sin between Him and myself. Learning to recognize my own sin was huge. I was so used to blaming others, I could not see my own sin. I had to take responsibility for the way I had responded to the abuse and sin of others in my past. The forgiveness I was withholding from others was just as sinful as the original sin itself. I have learned that holding on to any sin just gives the world, my flesh, and Satan an invitation to build on it.

In reference to the work of the Holy Spirit using Jeremiah 1:10, the Lord revealed to Lynne the acronym PLOW—Pray, Listen, Obey, and Wait. The acronym became her mantra throughout this phase of discipleship.

Reflecting on the truth she learned from Genesis 3, Lynne credits the power of the Holy Spirit as He revealed to her how she had allowed the emotions of shame, anger, and fear to control her life. She recalls, "I was controlled by my emotions and not by the truth of God's Word." Further, Lynne realized by examining Genesis 3 that danger exists in not knowing the Word of God, and she credits this as being instrumental in her listening to the wrong voice. She states, "I didn't even know I was listening to the wrong voice. That voice was so comfortable and familiar. It sounded like the truth."

She was able to see that the emotions of fear and anger were only the by-products of the sin of unforgiveness. She realized that the sin of her grandfather had caused her to respond with the sin of unforgiveness and bitterness, which she had covered, hidden, and blamed on others for years. When she retraced the sin to the voice to which she had been listening and compared it with the voice of the Lord, she realized the two did not align. At this point, Lynne had a choice to make. Which voice was she going to surrender her will to and obey?

Lynne had prayed for years about the situation but was only able to experience complete freedom from all the excess baggage she had carried when she chose to surrender her will and obey the Word of God. Realizing reconciliation must first occur with the Lord, she prayerfully confessed her sin of unforgiveness and allowed His faithfulness and righteousness to forgive and cleanse her (1 John 1:9). Likewise, in regard to reconciliation with her mother and father, Lynne specifically surrendered her will and obeyed Matthew 5:23–24, which states, "If therefore you are presenting your offering at the altar, and there remember that your brother has something against you, leave your offering there before the altar, and go your way; first be reconciled to your brother, and then come and present your offering." She met with her mother and asked for her forgiveness for the years of bitterness and resentment she had held. She contacted her father and asked for his forgiveness. Unaware that she had suffered in this manner, her father asked her for forgiveness for placing her in that situation. The Lord has restored fellowship in the family. In addition, Lynne has forgiven her grandfather. The freedom Lynne has experienced as a result of her surrendered will and obedience has been miraculously supernatural.

When asked to describe the relevance of God's Word in her life, Lynne replied, "God's Word is everything to me. It is truth. It is the basis for my life now. I now know I cannot live without the Word. I am learning to study the Word for myself. The Holy Spirit who lives in me is opening my eyes so that I can understand the Word and apply it to my life."

SADIE'S STORY

The first time I met Sadie was in my Sunday school class at church. As I recall the initial encounter, I remember her countenance appeared hard, angry, and sad. As I attempted to engage her in light conversation, I noticed her response was cold, distant, and defensive. As time progressed, it became apparent to me that Sadie's tough demeanor was merely an attempt to cover a life of immense pain, rejection, and abuse. In the weeks that followed, it was obvious that the Lord had sent Sadie to the class. The transformation that has occurred can best be told in her words. Just recently, Sadie shared her testimony in class because we were studying the Samaritan woman in John 4. The following testimony is what she shared.

> Looking back, my greatest sin was my unbelief and my open rebellion toward God because I didn't understand Him. I had not read the Word and, in fact, was not able to understand it when I had tried to read it. This all made more sense to me after I was saved as I read 2 Corinthians 4:3–4, which states, "And even if our gospel is veiled, it is veiled to those who are perishing, in whose case the god of this world has blinded the minds of the unbelieving, that they might not see the light of the gospel of the glory of Christ, who is the image of God."

> I thought I had been saved when, after much cajoling from my parents, at the age of thirteen I walked down the aisle to be baptized. Nothing happened and nothing changed. I married Robert when I was nineteen years old and found myself in an abusive marriage where I thought, *If only I do this or that, he will be nice to me.* I had a son in this marriage. The pregnancy and abuse took their toll on my health to the point of being told by my doctor to get my affairs in order. I left my husband because of the constant abuse, only to find myself cut off from the church in which I had grown up. They told me I was going to go to hell for leaving him. This caused me to dive into drinking to drown my sorrow.

> I had tried to take my life many times by drinking and had been brought back to life, only to hate the emergency room doctor who saved my life. I didn't know then that instead of the nothingness I had believed was on the other side, I would have found hell.

> Years later, I attended a series of behavior modification meetings to get help. I got sober and invented a "god as I understood him." During this time, I met and married my second husband, Peter. He ended up going to jail after trying to shoot some cops. I tried to cope by immersing myself into my job. I would work anywhere from 70 to 120 hours a week.

> I divorced again and married for a third time to a man named Don. He was a very loving husband. Life was good until the doctor told me that I had a serious illness that would require nine months of treatments. He could not assure me that I would be okay after the treatments. The medical treatments had been successful and put me in remission. At this time when I was receiving medical care, my neighbor and friend Sarah invited me to church. Although she had invited me numerous

times before, this time I accepted. At this church, I found friendship and love. Sadly, I did not find Jesus. I was earning a good living, attending my behavior modification classes regularly, and going to church. I thought my life was okay. My "god" was the one I understood. I was earning respectability and people thought well of me. I had both feet on wrong footing.

Don died. Financially I was okay, but inside I was devastated. I thought God owed me, so I went husband hunting to find another man like Don. I found and married Tim, only to realize later that he was looking for financial security. Fifteen months later I discovered, by accident as I was monitoring all computers for viruses, that Tim had been visiting hard porn sites, looking at locations for funeral homes and crematoriums, and researching information on how to break into trust funds. I found out he had been planning my death and the theft of my stepdaughter's inheritance, which Don had left for supervision in my name.

At this same time in my life, I had started attending First Baptist Church because it was close to my house. I can still recall the first time I heard the pastor's invitation at the end of the service. I laughed. I will never forget the Christmas message that year as I was confronted with my sin, my need for a Savior, and all that Jesus had done for me. This time I wasn't laughing. Instead, I remember the conviction I felt and the need to go home and pray. I knew that my choices had put me where I was, and for the first time in my life, I saw my open rebellion toward God. The gospel not only showed me the Savior; it revealed my need for one.

Unsure how to pray, and not knowing how to proceed, I remember asking God to give me a sign as to whether I should stay in this marriage or tell Tim to leave. I told the Lord that if at Christmas, Tim gave me a gift of any kind, I would take it that he was supposed to stay. But if he didn't give me a gift, I would know that God was telling me he needed to go. So when Christmas came, not only had Tim not gotten me a gift, but he actually opened the gifts others had given me. I knew God had heard, had answered, and was protecting me. I confronted Tim with all I had found, and he left for California. That day I fell to my knees, praying in thanks for my life. I asked for forgiveness for my sins, giving my life to Jesus as my Lord and Savior. That day, on December 25, 2010, my life changed dramatically. On January 9, 2011, I was baptized in Christ, my first act of obedience, and I started studying the Word in earnest.

A year later, I married my fifth husband, David. As I have gotten closer to Jesus, I have been experiencing rejection from my "friends" at the behavior modification classes. At first I couldn't understand it, but the Holy Spirit, through Scriptures, has made it clear that I was guilty of idolatry, harlotry, and having a heart of stone. I had looked to men and husbands to fill the place only God could fill. I was the woman at the well. In my behavior modification classes, my first sponsor once told me, "If anyone's brain needed washing, it's yours." I believed her. I have since learned through the Holy Spirit and the Scriptures that I didn't need brain washing; I needed a new heart. Ezekiel 36:26 states, "I will give you a new heart and put a new spirit within you; and I will remove the heart of stone from your flesh and give you a heart of flesh." I am so grateful to God the Father, Jesus Christ, and the Holy Spirit for all that was done for me.

In another act of obedience, I came to be discipled in the ways of Christian living. As we looked at Genesis 3, I saw my heart was filled with anger, guilt, shame, and fear. As I asked the Holy Spirit to lead me to the source of my anger, He brought to mind when my oldest brother had molested me as a child. I also carried a lot of guilt in regard to my niece. I had not warned her, and she, too, was molested by him. The Lord led me to contact my brother and ask for his forgiveness for the years of hatred, bitterness, and unforgiveness I had held in my heart toward him. He also led me to contact my niece and ask for her forgiveness for not warning her. To my surprise, I found out that my brother is a Christian. I also found out that he had been trying to contact me to ask for my forgiveness, but no one would give him my number. We were able to mutually forgive each other. There was immediate relief and healing. My niece, on the other hand, has chosen not to acknowledge my letter of apology but has been much friendlier since the letter was sent.

It hasn't always been easy, but it has been worth it. I've cried a million tears of pain and joy. I have learned that the peace and joy during the storm are worth far more to me than the testing. I cannot thank the Lord enough. As I have looked in Scripture for a way to say thanks to the Lord, He showed me 1 Timothy 1:12–14, which states, "I thank Christ Jesus our Lord, who has strengthened me, because He considered me faithful, putting me into service; even though I was formerly a blasphemer and a persecutor and a violent aggressor. And yet I was shown mercy, because I acted ignorantly in unbelief; and the grace of our Lord was more than abundant, with the faith and love which are found in Christ Jesus." For me, these verses say it all.

CONCLUSION

The personal vignettes that I have shared are merely a sampling of lives that have been transformed by the power of the Lord Jesus Christ. Although the stories are different, the characteristics are the same. Each of the women described the issue of spiritual immaturity using the symptoms defined in 1 John 2:12–14. Each woman confessed spiritual weakness, which was the result of having been overcome by the enemy with fortified strongholds such as anxiety, bitterness, unforgiveness, depression, idolatry, fear, and rejection. Even though each consistently remained in the church, and even some attained places of spiritual leadership, each woman confessed that the Word of God was not abiding within her in such a way as to result in transformation. All the women confessed that past Bible studies had been essentially informational rather than transformational. Each woman described the process of allowing the Spirit of God to take the Word of God to cut open spiritually infected areas. Although the areas were different, the solution was the same—surrendering one's will and obedience to the Word of God.

Likewise, each woman likened the process of "plucking up and destroying" to spiritual surgery. Each of the women was willing to be accountable to me as I guided her back to the Lord and His powerful, life-changing Word. As a result of their faith, healing occurred. When healing occurred, the women became hungry for His Word.

Two types of people do not eat: those who are physically sick and the dead. The same is true in the spiritual realm. The newfound spiritual hunger led to the second phase of the discipleship process: teaching others to study the Word for themselves, while establishing doctrinal foundations upon which to build and grow.

As for this workbook, I will forever be indebted to the Lord for giving me a biblical framework from which to disciple others (1 John 2:12–14) and providing a biblical framework from which to counsel (Gen. 3). And as He continues to bring women who are being overcome by the evil one, who are spiritually weak, and in whom the Word of God does not abide consistently, I will use the tools He has given me in this workbook to disciple them. In essence, I will point them to the Savior, Jesus Christ, and His Word.

My prayer is that He will use this workbook in the process of your spiritual transformation and in the lives of those He sends in your life to disciple. May He use this as a tool "for the equipping of the saints for the work of service, to the building up of the body of Christ; until we all attain to the unity of the faith, and of the knowledge of the Son of God, to a mature man, to the measure of the stature which belongs to the fulness of Christ" (Eph. 4:12–13). To God be the glory!

For more information concerning workshops, training, speaking engagements, or materials, please contact us at www.transformingtheheart@yahoo.com.

NOTES

INTERPRETATION OF 1 JOHN 2:12–14[101]

In 1 John 2:12–14, John provides an excellent diagnostic tool to help assess the spiritual maturity of believers. This is necessary for the accurate discipleship of others toward spiritual maturation. In 1 John 2:12, John qualifies the audience, calling them "little children" (teknion). The entire epistle is devoted to the teknion (with the exception of 1 John 2:13, 18). John describes this group as those whose "sins are forgiven . . . for His name's sake" (1 John 2:12). To interpret correctly, one must acknowledge the tense, mood, and voice of the verb "forgiven" as a perfect indicative passive verb.[102] The perfect tense can be defined as an action in the past with present and future results.[103] The passive voice indicates that the subject receives the action.[104] In other words, the forgiveness received by the little children is an act that occurred in the past (justification) but is in the process of having present (sanctification) and future (glorification) results. The passive voice is indicative of the fact that salvation is an act of God. Mankind is merely the recipient of this act of God's grace. Clearly, John is addressing those who have believed in Christ for salvation.

New Testament scholar Robert Yarbrough states, "The teknia (little children) of 2:12 are probably the entire readership, conceived of by John as children of God through their reception of the gospel. By extension, because of John's apostolic ministry to them, they are referred to affectionately as his 'little children.'"[105] Among the little children (teknion) emerge three distinct groups beginning with the most mature, fathers (patēres), and ending with the least mature, children (paidion). Some scholars do not see a distinction in the use of the terms "little children" (teknion) and "children" (paidion); however, for the reasons cited in the critical word section of my dissertation, the separation of terms into three distinct groupings is maintained.[106] Similarly, Gary M. Burge, New Testament scholar and professor, states, "I prefer to view the first title [teknion] as an address for all John's followers. This makes the best sense of the order of the names [fathers or patēres, young men or neaniskos, and children or paidion]."[107]

Therefore, with the distinction in mind, John addresses the spiritual fathers first. The third level of spiritual maturity is all-inclusive in the use of the term "father," described as one who has known "Him who has been from the beginning" (1 John 2:13–14). According to Stott, "The fathers have progressed into a deep communion with God."[108]

Burge further defines the fathers as "those who are more mature in the faith, whose spiritual maturity and experience reach back many years with a knowledge of God that is securely anchored in the past. It is their seasoned wisdom that makes for steadfast faith in the present circumstances."[109] Moreover, discipleship must be both relational and intentional to be effective. In correlating directly the term "fathers" with "mothers," Randy Stinson, former dean of the School of Church Ministries at Southern Seminary, states, "Many women are involved in multiple Bible studies but have no personal mentor in their life who can speak redemptively to her and offer the instruction, encouragement, and correction that is so crucial for spiritual formation and the development of a godly pattern of life."[110] Therefore, spiritual mothers are essential in this reproductive process of making disciples.

The second level of maturity delineated by John is the young men (1 John 2:14). The young men have three defining characteristics. They are described as being "strong," and "the word of God abides in [them], and [they] have overcome the evil one" (1 John 2:14). The word "abide" literally means to "remain or to dwell."[111] The verb tense is present indicative active, meaning a continual dwelling or lifestyle. In other words, obedience to the Word of God is the habit of the young man's life. Furthermore, the young man is enabled by the Spirit to overcome the evil one in his obedience to the Word of God. The young man is not merely one who is in the Word; rather, the Word is in him. One can be in the Word of God and simply walk away with information. However, when the Word of God is in the man, transformation is the result. In reference to what makes the young man strong and able to overcome the enemy, it is that the Word of God abides in him. The Word is the difference maker.

Stedman describes the young man: "Young men are not fully mature. They are spiritual, but they are not mature. They still lack the full range of Christian experience. There is a difference between spirituality and maturity. Maturity is the final goal, and spirituality is the process by which you get there."[112]

Concerning the third level of spiritual maturity is the little children, or *paidion*, who "know the Father" (1 John 2:13). The word "know" is the Greek word *ginosko*. The difference in experiential knowledge between the fathers and the children is in the subject. In other words, "little children" (*paidion*)—the subject—know the Father in the same way an infant would know his parents. Their knowledge is limited. Just as an infant knows the voice of his father or that the father will provide what is needed, his knowledge of the father is limited because of his level of maturity.

Upon observation of the text and with regard to the contextual interpretation concerning the three stages of spiritual maturity within the body, one may correctly assume that what is true of the young men is not yet evident in the little children. For instance, rather than being strong in the faith, little children are spiritually weak. Rather than abiding in the Word and allowing the Word to abide in them, they are immature in the Word. Such immaturity in the Word can prove detrimental to the spiritual growth of the little children, making them susceptible to the false teachings and doctrines of the world. Understanding the severity connected to the little children's immaturity, Paul warns the church in Ephesus, "We are no longer to be children, tossed here and there by waves, and carried about by every wind of doctrine, by the trickery of men, by craftiness in deceitful scheming; but speaking the truth in love, we are to grow up in all aspects into Him, who is the head, even Christ" (Eph. 4:14–15). Not only is the warning against false teaching within these verses, but they also contain the command for growth in Christ, who is the living Word. Echoing the warnings of Paul, John counsels the little children, or *paidia*, concerning the coming antichrists. As their spiritual father, John understands his little children's vulnerability to the enemy's schemes because they are both weak and immature in the Word (1 John 2:18).

Similar to the manner in which the young man is strong, abiding in the Word, and able to overcome the enemy, the fathers maintain the same qualities and are also willing and able to reproduce them in others through evangelism and discipleship. The term "fathers" implies reproduction, responsibility, and maturity. Every spiritual leader in the church should fit in the category of the father (1 Tim. 3:2; Titus 1:9; 1 Pet. 5:2–3).

The difference maker in each stage of maturity is twofold: (1) one's absolute reliance on the Holy Spirit and (2) one's faith in the Word of God. Expounding on the irreplaceable work of the Spirit, Oswald Chambers states, "The Holy Ghost is the One who honours Jesus, and therein lies the essential necessity of receiving Him. 'He shall glorify Me,' said Jesus. The Holy Spirit does not glorify Christ-likeness, because Christ-likeness can be imitated; He glorifies Christ. It is impossible to imitate Jesus Christ." [113] According to Chambers, spiritual maturity or Christlikeness is "the absolute Self-surrender and Self-sacrifice of the Lord Jesus to the will of His Father . . . and the fullest meaning of sanctification is that Jesus Christ is 'made unto us sanctification,' that is, He creates in us what He is Himself."[114] For the spiritual father, absolute dependence on the power of the Holy Spirit is not only essential but is a way of life.

Likewise, one's faith in the Word of God is crucial in the process of spiritual maturation. Praying to the Father just before His death, Jesus stated, "Sanctify them in the truth, Thy word is truth" (John 17:17). According to the Lord Jesus, the means whereby one is sanctified is the Word of God. Paul stated, "I am not ashamed of the gospel, for it is the power of God for salvation" (Rom. 1:16). Notice Paul does not say that the gospel contains power for salvation; rather, *the gospel is the power for salvation*. Oftentimes, this verse is used to describe justification before an Almighty God. This is true. However, sanctification is the process whereby one is being saved from the power of sin. Therefore, the Word of God is the power of God for sanctification. The Word of God is inherently sufficient and does not need man's latest theory or psychological evaluation to aid in the process of salvation. All that is necessary for man is a faith that surrenders one's will and obeys the Word of God. Therein, one matures. Chambers states, "Spiritual maturity is not reached by the passing of years, but by obedience to the will of God."[115]

The spiritual father knows and understands this truth very well. His dependence is not on his knowledge or the wisdom of another. His knowledge rests in Christ alone and in His Word alone. To separate the Lord of the Word from the Word of the Lord is a mistake. Chambers states, "Our Lord Jesus Christ, the Word of God, and the Bible, the words of God, stand or fall together, they can never be separated without fatal results."[116] For those whose complete reliance is on the Holy Spirit, who are daily surrendering their wills and obeying the Word, growth and transformation occur.

In conclusion, John is not only providing a diagnostic tool for spiritual maturity but also giving the instructions, through the characteristics defined, on how to proceed to the next level of spiritual maturity. The assessment tool provided in John's epistle is a necessary part of disciple-making. As Stedman so aptly points out, "There is always room and provision for babies in the family circle. But Christians who are still babies after ten, twenty, thirty, even forty years of Christian life, these are the problems. They are immature and refuse to grow up."[117] If this phenomenon were occurring in the physical realm, one would diagnose an abnormality and be seeking medical attention as well as a cure. Thankfully, for every spiritual abnormality and deficit, a Great Physician is available, and His Word is the cure.

ENDNOTES

1 Joyce J. Fitzpatrick and Meredith Kazer, *The Encyclopedia of Nursing Research* (New York: Springer Publishing Co., 2006), 193.

2 Kristine Krapp and Jeffery Wilson, eds., *The Gale Encyclopedia of Children's Health*, vol. 2 (Detroit: Thompson Gale Publishing, 2005), 721.

3 Ibid., 722.

4 Jim Berg, *Changed into His Image* (Greenville, SC: Bob Jones University Press, 2000), 11.

5 Max Barnett, "One on One with God," accessed October 15, 2021, http://www.discipleshiplibrary.com/search.php?a=0&e=1&m=0&n=0&p=0&s=last_name&t=LAST%20 NAME.

6 W. E. Vine, *Vine's Expository Dictionary of Old and New Testament Words* (Grand Rapids: Fleming H. Revell, 1981), 316.

7 John MacArthur Jr., "Rediscovering Biblical Counseling," accessed October 2, 2013, http://articles.ochristian.com/article2279.shtml.

8 John MacArthur Jr., *Strange Fire* (Nashville: Nelson Books, 2013), xii.

9 Harold L. Wilmington, *Wilmington's Guide to the Bible* (Wheaton, IL: Tyndale House Publishers, 1984), 656–657.

10 C. F. H. Henry, *God, Revelation and Authority, Volume 4* (Wheaton, IL: Crossway Books, 1999), 266.

11 Ibid., 273.

12 J. E. Rosscup, "The Priority of Prayer and Expository Preaching," in *Rediscovering Expository Preaching* by John MacArthur Jr. (Dallas: Word Publishing, 1992), 105.

13 Vine, *Vine's Expository Dictionary*, 316.

14 Ibid., 71.

[15] Zodhiates, *Complete Word Study Dictionary*, 970.

[16] David Platt, *Follow Me* (Carol Stream, IL: Tyndale House Publishers, 2013), 19.

[17] Thomas Watson, *The Doctrine of Repentance* (Edinburg: The Banner of Truth Trust, 2012).

[18] Richard Owen Roberts, *Repentance: The First Word of the Gospel* (Wheaton, IL: Crossway, 2002).

[19] John MacArthur Jr., *The Gospel According to Jesus* (Grand Rapids, MI: Zondervan, 2008), 37.

[20] David Platt, *A Call to Die. A Call to Live: Follow Me* (Carol Stream, IL: Tyndale House Publishers, 2013), 6.

[21] Ibid.

[22] Ibid.

[23] J.D. Greear, *Stop Asking Jesus into Your Heart: How to Know for Sure You Are Saved* (Nashville: B & H Publishing, 2013), 5.

[24] Zodhiates, *The Complete Word Study Dictionary*, 900.

[25] Zodhiates, 374.

[26] John MacArthur Jr., *The MacArthur New Testament Commentary: Matthew 1–7* (Chicago: Moody Press, 1985), 479.

[27] Rosaria Champagne Butterfield, *The Secret Thoughts of an Unlikely Convert* (Pittsburgh, PA: Crown & Covenant Publications, 2012), 2.

[28] Ibid., 1.

[29] Ibid., 81.

[30] Vine, *Vine's Expository Dictionary*, 316.

[31] Kay Arthur, "Freed from Sin's Penalty," *Romans Part 1, Precept Upon Precept Inductive Series* (Chattanooga, TN: Precept Ministries International, 1995), 139.

[32] Wayne Grudem, *Systematic Theology* (Grand Rapids, MI: Zondervan, 1994), 724.

[33] Ibid., 746.

[34] J. K. Grider, "Glorification," *The Evangelical Dictionary of Theology*, ed. Walter A. Elwell, 2nd ed.

(Grand Rapids, MI: Baker Academics, 2001), 484.

[35] Zodhiates, *The Complete Word Study New Testament*, 940.

36 W. Arndt, F. W. Danker, and W. Bauer, *A Greek-English Lexicon of the New Testament and Other Early Christian Literature,* 3rd ed. (Chicago: University of Chicago Press, 2000), 749.

37 Zodhiates, *The Complete Word Study Dictionary,* 373.

38 Ibid., 892.

39 For a more academic and detailed approach to this passage, consider the biblical interpretation offered in a previous work titled *Developing a Biblical Model to Disciple Women in the Process of Spiritual Maturation,* located in the Appendix.

40 Cressey, M. H., "Knowledge," in D. R. W. Wood, I. H. Marshall, A. R. Millard, J. I. Packer, and D. J. Wiseman (eds.), *New Bible Dictionary,* 3rd ed. (Leicester, England; Downers Grove, IL: InterVarsity Press, 1996), 657.

41 Kathleen Sheeder-Bonanno, "Death Barged In," accessed October 15, 2021, https://poets.org/poem/death-barged. Used with permission.

42 Howley, G. C. D., "Evil," in D. R. W. Wood, I. H. Marshall, A. R. Millard, J. I. Packer, and D. J. Wiseman (eds.), *New Bible dictionary,* 3rd ed (Leicester, England; Downers Grove, IL: InterVarsity Press, 1996), 348.

43 Spiros Zodhiates, *The Complete Word Study Dictionary New Testament* (Chattanooga, TN: AMG Publishers, 1993), 809.

44 Howley, G. C. D., "Evil," in D. R. W. Wood, I. H. Marshall, A. R. Millard, J. I. Packer, and D. J. Wiseman (eds.), *New Bible dictionary,* 3rd ed (Leicester, England; Downers Grove, IL: InterVarsity Press, 1996), 348.

45 Richard Owen Roberts, *Repentance: The First Word of the Gospel* (Wheaton, IL: Crossway, 2002), 150.

46 Ibid., 195.

47 Ibid., 195.

48 Thomas Watson, first published 1663, *A Divine Cordial,* reprinted as *All Things for Good* (Edinburgh: The Banner of Truth Trust, 1986), 34.

49 Derek Prime, *Created to Praise* (Ross-shire, Scotland: Derek Prime Christian Focus Publications Ltd., 2013), 84.

50 Zodhiates, *The Complete New Testament Word Study,* 895.

51 Spiros Zodhiates, *The Complete Word Study Dictionary New Testament* (Chattanooga, TN: AMG Publishers, 1992), 1437.

52 Tedd Tripp, *Shepherding a Child's Heart* (Wapwallopen, PA: Shepherd Press, 1995), xx.

[53] Tripp, *Shepherding a Child's Heart*, 54.

[54] John MacArthur Jr., *The MacArthur New Testament Commentary: 2 Corinthians* (Chicago: Moody Publishers, 2003), 328.

[55] Zodhiates, *The Complete Word Study New Testament*, 918.

[56] All the information regarding the Inductive Method is taken from the Precept Bible Study Method and has been derived from over twenty years of training and leading Precept studies. Further inquiries into the Precept method of training can be made at Precept Ministries International at www.Precept.org.

[57] Ibid.

[58] All the information regarding Bible Study Fellowship (BSF) is derived from four years of participation and leadership within the organization. Further information regarding BSF can be found at www.bsfinternational.org.

[59] Further inquiries into the Precept method of training can be made at Precept Ministries International at www.Precept.org.

[60] The answers are as follows: a. Jesus is speaking; b. to His disciples. Please note that this is the correct biblical interpretation; however, the verse is applicable to you and me today as well.

[61] Answers to question #5: (1) **What** is Mary doing? (2) To **what** is Mary listening? And (3) **Where** is Mary?

[62] The answers: (1) Worried; (2) Bothered by many things.

[63] The three things contrasted are (1) the sister's choice when Jesus was present; (2) the Lord's evaluation of each choice; and (3) the necessary choice: the many things versus the one thing.

[64] Zodhiates, *Word Study New Testament*.

[65] Zodhiates, *The Word Study Dictionary*, 1400.

[66] Ibid., 113.

[67] Ibid., 1149.

[68] Ibid., 227.

[69] Zodhiates, *The Word Study Dictionary*, 961.

[70] Ibid., 1400.

[71] Ibid., 544.

[72] I. H. Marshall. *The Gospel of Luke: A Commentary on the Greek Text. New International Greek Testament Commentary* (Exeter: Paternoster Press, 1978), 452.

[73] R. H. Stein, *The New American Commentary: Luke*, vol. 24 (Nashville: Broadman & Holman Publishers, 1992), 321.

[74] Ibid.

[75] T. C. Butler, *Holman New Testament Commentary: Luke*, vol. 3 (Nashville: Broadman & Holman Publishers, 2000), 173.

[76] John MacArthur Jr., *The MacArthur New Testament Commentary: Luke 6–10* (Chicago: Moody Press, 2011), 364.

[77] Ibid., 365.

[78] Ibid., 366.

[79] Oswald Chambers, *My Utmost for His Highest Journal*, January 18 entry.

[80] Alistair Begg, "First Things First," *The Gospel According to Luke, Volume 4*, sermon #2141, accessed January 20, 2014, http://www.truthforlife.org.

[81] Ibid.

[82] Ibid.

[83] Ibid.

[84] For study helps, see the chapter in this workbook titled "The Word of God Abides Within."

[85] All the word studies were done with the help of Spiros Zodhiates, *The Complete New Testament Word Study* and *New Testament Dictionary* (Chattanooga, TN: AMG Publishers, 1992 and 1993 respectively).

[86] S. K. Weber, *Holman New Testament Commentary: Matthew*, vol. 1 (Nashville: Broadman & Holman Publishers, 2000), 196.

[87] MacArthur, *The Gospel According to Jesus*, 132.

[88] Ibid., 131.

[89] Ibid., 133.

[90] Leon Morris, *The Pillar New Testament Commentary: The Gospel According to Matthew* (Grand Rapids, MI; Leicester, England: W.B. Eerdmans; InterVarsity Press, 1992), 346–347.

[91] MacArthur, *The Gospel According to Jesus*, 133.

92 Zodhiates, *The Complete Word Study Dictionary New Testament*, 627.

93 Zodhiates, *The Complete Word Study Dictionary New Testament*, 709.

94 Ibid., 134.

95 Zodhiates, *The Complete Word Study New Testament Dictionary*, 815.

96 MacArthur, *The Gospel According to Jesus*, 135.

97 Ibid.

98 Ibid., 136.

99 Arthur Pink, *Spiritual Growth in Grace, or Christian Progress* (Bellingham, WA: Logos Bible Software, 2005).

100 Charles H. Spurgeon, *Farm Sermons,* "The Parable of the Sower," accessed July 22, 2014, http://www.spurgeon.org/misc/sower.htm.

101 The following excerpt is not exhaustive; however, I pray it will add clarity and cause you to consider your personal role as a disciple and the biblical mandate to make disciples. It is taken from a previous work titled *Developing a Biblical Model to Disciple Women in the Process of Spiritual Maturation* (Fort Worth, TX: Southwestern Baptist Theological Seminary, 2013), 32–34.

102 Zodhiates, *The Complete Word Study Dictionary, New Testament,* Word Study Series (Chattanooga, TN: AMG Publishing, 1993), 788.

103 Ibid., 866.

104 Ibid.

105 Robert W. Yarbrough, *1–3 John: Baker Exegetical Commentary* (Grand Rapids, MI: Baker Academics, 2008), 114.

106 Melinda Clark, *Developing a Biblical Model to Disciple Women in the Process of Spiritual Maturation* (Fort Worth, TX: Southwestern Baptist Theological Seminary, 2013), 32–38.

107 Gary M. Burge, *Letters of John: NIV Application Commentary,* ed. Terry Muck (Grand Rapids, MI: Zondervan , 1996), 111.

108 John R. W. Stott, *The Epistles of John.* Tyndale New Testament Commentaries (Grand Rapids, MI: William B. Eerdmans Publishing Co., 1981).

109 Burge, *Letters of John,* 113.

110 Randy Stinson and Timothy Paul Jones, eds., *Trained in the Fear of God: Family Ministry in Theological, Historical, and Practical Perspective* (Grand Rapids, MI: Kregel Publications, 2011), 84.

[111] Zodhiates, *The Complete Word Study Dictionary New Testament*, 959.

[112] Ray C. Stedman, *Expository Studies in 1 John* (Waco, TX: Word Books, 1980), 90.

[113] Oswald Chambers, *The Complete Works of Oswald Chambers* (Grand Rapids, MI: Discovery House Publishers, 2000), 476.

[114] Ibid., 236.

[115] Ibid., 221.

[116] Ibid., 271.

[117] Stedman, *Expository Studies in 1 John*, 84.

BIBLIOGRAPHY

Arndt, W., F. W. Danker, and W. Bauer, *A Greek-English Lexicon of the New Testament and Other Early Christian Literature,* 3rd ed. Chicago: University of Chicago Press, 2000.

Barnett, Max. "One on One with God." Accessed October 15, 2021, http://www.discipleshiplibrary.com/search.php?a=0&e=1&m=0&n=0&p=0&s=last_name&t=LAST%20NAME.

Begg, Alistair. "First Things First." *The Gospel According to Luke, Volume 4,* sermon #2141. Accessed January 20, 2014, http://www.truthforlife.org.

Berg, Jim. *Changed into His Image.* Greenville, SC: Bob Jones University Press, 2000.

Burge, Gary M. *Letters of John: NIV Application Commentary,* ed. Terry Muck. Grand Rapids: Zondervan Publishing House, 1996.

Butler, T. C. *Holman New Testament Commentary: Luke,* vol. 3. Nashville, TN: Broadman & Holman Publishers, 2000.

Butterfield, Rosaria Champagne, *The Secret Thoughts of an Unlikely Convert.* Pittsburg, PA: Crown & Covenant Publications, 2012.

Chambers, Oswald. *The Complete Works of Oswald Chambers.* Grand Rapids, MI: Discovery House Publishers, 2000.

Chambers, Oswald. *My Utmost for His Highest Journal.* January 18 entry.

Clark, Melinda. *Developing a Biblical Model to Disciple Women in the Process of Spiritual Maturation.*

Fort Worth, TX: Southwestern Baptist Theological Seminary, 2013.

Fitzpatrick, Joyce J. and Meredith Kazer, *The Encyclopedia of Nursing Research.* New York: Springer Publishing Co., 2006.

Greear, J.D. *Stop Asking Jesus into Your Heart: How to Know for Sure You Are Saved.* Nashville, B & H Publishing, 2013.

Henry, C. F. H. *God, Revelation and Authority, Volume 4*. Wheaton, IL: Crossway Books, 1999.

Krapp, Kristine and Jeffery Wilson, eds., *The Gale Encyclopedia of Children's Health*, vol. 2. Detroit: Thompson Gale Publishing, 2005.

MacArthur, John Jr. *The Gospel According to Jesus*. Grand Rapids: Zondervan, 2008.

MacArthur, John Jr. *The MacArthur New Testament Commentary: Matthew 1–7*. Chicago: Moody Press, 1985.

MacArthur, John Jr. *The MacArthur New Testament Commentary: Luke 6–10*. Chicago: Moody Press, 2011. MacArthur, John Jr. *The MacArthur New Testament Commentary: 2 Corinthians*. Chicago: Moody Publishers, 2003.

MacArthur, John Jr. "Rediscovering Biblical Counseling." Accessed October 15, 2021, http://articles.ochristian.com/article2279.shtml.

MacArthur, John Jr. *Strange Fire*. Nashville: Nelson Books, 2013.

Marshall, I. H. *The Gospel of Luke: A Commentary on the Greek Text. New International Greek Testament Commentary*. Exeter: Paternoster Press, 1978.

Morris, Leon. *The Pillar New Testament Commentary: The Gospel According to Matthew*. Grand Rapids, MI; Leicester, England: W.B. Eerdmans; InterVarsity Press, 1992.

Pink, Arthur. *Spiritual Growth in Grace, or Christian Progress*. Bellingham, WA: Logos Bible Software, 2005.

Platt, David. *Follow Me*. Carol Stream, IL: Tyndale House Publishers, 2013.

Prime, Derek. *Created to Praise*. Ross-shire, Scotland: Derek Prime Christian Focus Publications Ltd., 2013.

Roberts, Richard Owen. *Repentance: The First Word of the Gospel*. Wheaton, IL, Crossway, 2002.

Rosscup, J. E. "The Priority of Prayer and Expository Preaching." In *Rediscovering Expository Preaching* by John MacArthur. Dallas: Word Publishing, 1992.

Spurgeon, Charles H. *Farm Sermons*, "The Parable of the Sower." https://www.amazon.com/Farm-Sermons-C-H-Spurgeon/dp/1672492459/ref=tmm_pap_swatch_0?_encoding=UTF8&qid=&sr=#detailBullets_feature_div.

Stedman, Ray C. *Expository Studies in 1 John*. Waco, TX: Word Books, 1980.

Stein, R. H. *The New American Commentary: Luke*, vol. 24. Nashville: Broadman & Holman Publishers, 1992.

Stinson, Randy and Timothy Paul Jones, eds., *Trained in the Fear of God: Family Ministry in Theological, Historical, and Practical Perspective*. Grand Rapids: Kregel Publications, 2011.

Stott, John R. W. *The Epistles of John.* Tyndale New Testament Commentaries. Grand Rapids, MI: William B. Eerdmans Publishing Co.

Tripp, Tedd. *Shepherding a Child's Heart.* Wapwallopen, PA: Shepherd Press, 1995.

Vine, W. E. *Vine's Expository Dictionary of Old and New Testament Words.* Grand Rapids: Fleming H. Revell, 1981.

Watson, Thomas. First published 1663, *A Divine Cordial.* Reprinted as *All Things for Good.* Edinburgh: The Banner of Truth Trust, 1986.

Watson, Thomas. First published in 1668, *The Doctrine of Repentance.* Edinburg: The Banner of Truth Trust, 2012.

Weber, S. K. *Holman New Testament Commentary: Matthew,* vol. 1. Nashville, TN: Broadman & Holman Publishers, 2000.

Wilmington, Harold L. *Wilmington's Guide to the Bible.* Wheaton, IL: Tyndale House Publishers, 1984.

Yarbrough, Robert W. *1–3 John: Baker Exegetical Commentary.* Grand Rapids, MI: Baker Academics, 2008. Zodhiates, Spiros. *The Complete New Testament Dictionary.* Chattanooga: AMG Publishers, 1993.

Zodhiates, Spiros. *The Complete New Testament Word Study.* Chattanooga: AMG Publishers, 1992.

WALKING HAND IN HAND AS CHRIST'S LOVE
transforms lives

AMG | MEETING THE
INTERNATIONAL | **DEEPEST NEEDS**

WE BELIEVE THE GOSPEL IS TRANSFORMATIVE

And you can change the world one child at a time.

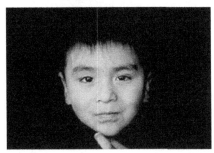

Thousands of children in the world are born into a cycle of poverty that has been around for generations, leaving them without hope for a safe and secure future. For a little more than $1 a day you can provide the tools a child needs to break the cycle in the name of Jesus.

OUR CONTACT

 423-894-6060
 info@amginternational.org

 @amgintl
 6815 Shallowford Rd. Chattanooga, TN 37421

Made in the USA
Middletown, DE
13 February 2022

61027983R00099